KEN LAYNE
DESERT ORACLE

Ken Layne publishes *Desert Oracle* and hosts its companion radio show and podcast from a haunted old compound in the Great Mojave Wilderness, one of four American deserts he has called home.

He loves all the desert creatures, but especially the local gopher snakes, ravens, coyotes, and antelope ground squirrels.

Find out more, if you must, at KenLayne.com and DesertOracle.com.

DESERT ORACLE

MCD | PICADOR | FARRAR, STRAUS AND GIROUX | NEW YORK

DESERT ORACLE

VOLUME 1:
Strange True Tales from the American Southwest

KEN LAYNE

MCD
Picador
120 Broadway, New York 10271

Copyright © 2020 by Ken Layne
All rights reserved
Printed in the United States of America
Originally published in 2020 by MCD / Farrar, Straus and Giroux
First paperback edition, 2021

Much of this material first appeared, in various forms, in *Desert Oracle*, issues 1–8, 2015–2019, and on *Desert Oracle Radio*, 2017–2019.
Portions of "Pahranagat Man" were originally published in the *Desert Sun*'s *Desert Magazine*, September 2019.
"Edward Abbey's Ode to Solitude" was originally published in the *Los Angeles Times* Books and Ideas section, January 2018.
"Try Not to Die" was originally published in *Palm Springs Life*, September 2019.
"Hidden Cities and Secret Creatures of Death Valley" was commissioned by the Mojave Project.

Desert Southwest space-break ornaments by Tim the Finn / Shutterstock.com.
Owing to limitations of space, photograph credits can be found on page 289.

The Library of Congress has cataloged the MCD hardcover edition as follows:
Names: Layne, Ken, 1965– author.
Title: Desert oracle : volume 1 : strange true tales from the American Southwest / Ken Layne.
Other titles: Strange true tales from the American Southwest | Desert oracle.
Description: First edition. | New York : MCD / Farrar, Straus and Giroux, 2020.
Identifiers: LCCN 2020028194 | ISBN 9780374139681 (hardcover)
Subjects: LCSH: Curiosities and wonders—Mojave Desert. | Mojave Desert—Description and travel. | Mojave Desert—History. | Mojave Desert—Miscellanea.
Classification: LCC F868.M65 L397 2020 | DDC 979.4/95—dc23
LC record available at https://lccn.loc.gov/2020028194

Paperback ISBN: 978-1-250-80035-0

Designed by Gretchen Achilles

Our books may be purchased in bulk for promotional, educational, or business use. Please contact your local bookseller or the Macmillan Corporate and Premium Sales Department at 1-800-221-7945, extension 5442, or by email at MacmillanSpecialMarkets@macmillan.com.

Picador® is a U.S. registered trademark and is used by Macmillan Publishing Group, LLC, under license from Pan Books Limited.

For book club information, please visit facebook.com/picadorbookclub or email marketing@picadorusa.com.

mcdbooks.com • Follow us on Twitter, Facebook, and Instagram at @mcdbooks
picadorusa.com • Instagram: @picador • Twitter and Facebook: @picadorusa

3 5 7 9 10 8 6 4

For the good people who love and protect the desert wilderness

CONTENTS

Introduction 3

Try Not to Die 9

The Known Unknown: Tales of Yucca Man 19

The Boy Who Vanished 33

Ravens 37

Doc Springer's Last Word in Health: Zzyzx 41

Horror of the Solar Lodge 47

Eulogy for a Space Mission 57

The White Stag 63

Apostle of the Cacti 67

Fighting Hitler and Defending the Desert 71

The Hermit Ballerina 75

Outlaw in the Rocks 83

Magic and War in Los Alamos with
William S. Burroughs 87

The Landers Earthquake 97

Hidden Cities and Secret Creatures of Death Valley 105

Marty Robbins on the Cowboy Trail from
Phoenix to El Paso 119

Edward Abbey's Ode to Solitude	125
Rambling Around with Ed Abbey	133
Scary Stories Around the Campfire	147
Pahranagat Man: Area 51's Ancient Monster	159
Cowboys and Poets	177
A Day Hike to Hell and Back	181
Philosophy on the Rocks	187
The Murder King of Western Swing	191
La Llorona Is Coming to Drown All the Children	219
Wonder Valley	227
When Eisenhower Met the Space Aliens	233
The Krill Papers	239
Dr. Jaeger's Hibernating Bird	247
The Devil (?) in Amboy Crater	255
When the Nights Were Weird: Art Bell and the Kingdom of Nye	263
The Governor's Space Alien	269
Broadcasts from Beyond	275
Acknowledgments	285

DESERT
ORACLE

INTRODUCTION

Within these pages are many mysteries of the desert. Some are cruel and terrible, others sublime, and a persistent few remain inexplicable by our current metrics of understanding.

Desert is wilderness stripped bare, and when left alone is creation in perfection. The landscape is vast and visible, the geology raw and exposed, the plants and animals in ideal proportion. Fresh water is generally in limited supply, but that has never stopped life from thriving in lands of little rain.

Our own species has always been fond of these harsh, arid places. The first civilizations rose up from desert sands: Mesopotamia, ancient Egypt, the Indus Valley. The wilderness of antiquity was wild desert. And that's where our philosophers and prophets went to meditate on mountaintops, to abandon society for a while and sleep under the stars or within limestone caves.

There were many river-valley civilizations in the North American desert, too, before our current mess of outlet malls and cell towers and interstates: the

Hohokam in the Salt River Valley, beneath modern Phoenix; the ancient Pueblo culture of the Four Corners. The Taos Pueblo is a rare unbroken link to those varied pasts. Despite the plastic letters on the gas stations and the same banal television programming beamed or streamed into every home, Taos is more or less as it was when Hernando de Alvarado arrived some five centuries ago, and as it had been centuries earlier, when the Roman church was still struggling to Christianize the diverse peoples of Europe.

Through a combination of accident and intent, much of the American desert remains mostly intact, mostly wild. The accident was in the claiming of so much American territory by the U.S. federal government in the mid-1800s, actions taken to prevent competing claims and occupation by Spain, Mexico, France, England, Russia, all our old imperial rivals. Places with surface water attracted settlers, despite the heat and sandstorms and scorpions, while the vast walls of mountains and expanses of dry lakes and valleys were spared much permanent development. This was followed by dramatic efforts to preserve and protect these desert ecosystems as national parks and monuments and federally designated wilderness, actions inspired by the nature mystics of American transcendentalism. In the twenty-first century, conservationists aim to save what they can of entire ecosystems, and not just photogenic islands of flora and fauna surrounded by industrial mining and eroded cattle range. Even without the dense forests we associate with the crucial storage of carbon on this planet, wild desert forms an immense "carbon sink" over a third of our planet's landmass, from the ancient aquifers beneath the parched surface to the vast networks of microbiotic crust that bind the desert together.

This is a simplified explanation to a complex question—*Why is so much of the American desert held in public trust?*—and is not intended to negate the intentional horrors visited upon indigenous cultures, the wide-scale extermination of desert species, or the determined efforts today by humanity-hating fanatics to reverse our limited protections of this earthly paradise.

When you are in the great desert wilderness, you must carry some understanding of why it's still that way, why it's so contrary to the numbing sprawl of our current civilization. It's the way it is because people spent lifetimes fighting to keep it that way, suffering more defeats than victories, because when you love a place that is what you do.

If this landscape affects your soul in this manner, you may have no choice but to join the noble and holy effort. We could use the help, whether you become a park ranger or join the Green New Deal conservation corps or volunteer a couple of times per year to clean up a nature preserve or lead schoolkids on backcountry hiking trips.

You might even need to become an outlaw, a hero. We are not so far away from the old times of adventure,

of great deeds. Do not fall into the trap of anxiety and emptiness. There is purpose waiting out here, for anyone who comes in honest pursuit of it.

A revelation in the desert is available, in our time. It may fit a practice or theology you bring along with your water and walking stick and beer cans and yoga mat, or it may shatter your psyche entirely. Both are worth the effort, worth the trouble, worth going where few others travel, worth leaving behind the dull comforts of tourist resorts and constant connection. Some people see the face of God (whoever she is) blasting light beams into their brains on the desert highway. Some people fall off a boulder and spend days wondering if they'll live or die (it's always one or the other). I have witnessed pure wild joy on a fellow human's face simply because there was no telephone signal available, no electronic-map display to show the nearest cluster of coffee and hamburger chains. Freedom, finally.

Out here, beyond the robotic grip of a civilization in disarray and despair, I promise you will feel human again, if only for a little while. Should this experience of old wonder appeal to you, then you will be back as often as possible, and you may have no choice but to call the desert home. And if it's home, you have no choice but to defend it.

There's nothing more fun than a purpose in life.

TRY NOT TO DIE

It wasn't supposed to go like this, wasn't the plan at all. The plan was to get out of town for a few days and explore the desert. Fill up the Instagram feed with abandoned gas stations and cracked asphalt two-lanes snaking through forests of Joshua trees. Beers at a roadhouse, impulse buys at a boutique on Highway 62, a night under the stars from the safety of an Airbnb hot tub or campfire ring.

And now it's a late summer day, well over a hundred degrees, not a stylish swimming pool or outdoor cocktail bar in sight. You've been sitting in the car, the doors flung open, the burning air wrapped around you, suffocating and dense and so very dry. An empty cardboard coffee cup in the drink holder. An empty plastic water bottle crumpled under the seat. It is midday. Which means, in seven or eight hours the ball of orange fire in the sky will finally sink behind the mountains and the temperature will sink down to ninety-five degrees or so, if you're lucky.

Something gave out, the gas in the tank or the city tires or the transmission or maybe the rear axle, snapped in two by a boulder partially buried in the sand on this godforsaken dirt road you never meant to be on, never consciously chose to take at all. The voice of the navigation robot was as sure as ever: "Turn right at the gas station," even though there was little left of that particular gas station, and the road itself was forlorn and untroubled by recent tire tracks. There was something you were headed for, an art exhibit on the open desert, a historic mining site, a location from a television show you remembered, a sweeping view of the national monument. It doesn't matter now. Unless you write it down, nobody will ever know why you wound up dead on a rough sandy track that could charitably be called a jeep trail.

Even if they find your remains, which might not happen for years, your personal story will not be told. Maybe there will be a local news article somewhere. "Human Remains Found Hours from Nearest Settlement," that kind of thing. If anybody remembers you, maybe they'll clip it out of the newspaper, bookmark the website page. You had so much life left to live, so many things you never got around to doing. And now all you're going to do is become a sunbaked skeleton picked over by vultures and ants, one bony hand stretched out ahead. Maybe at the end, you thought you were almost home.

The Mojave Desert covers much of Southern California and a bit of the neighboring states: southern Nevada, the Arizona strip, the bottom corner of Utah. Before this dried-out expanse of burnt-chocolate mountains and blinding playas and lonely roads became beautiful in the eyes of the beautiful people, it was something to endure on the way to Las Vegas or the Colorado River, or something to survive on the way to whatever was luring you to the West Coast.

There were always desert rats, always the antisocial sort who looked at this punishing landscape and felt at home. The romantics, the people who required a weird backdrop to fit their personal movie. But there were never enough of them to fill many hotel rooms or vacation rentals. And so the desert was mostly ignored, unless the steady jobs of the Los Angeles Basin were in commuting distance. Unless a corporation gets ahold of some government desert land to use for giant solar towers or windmills or a gold mine or some insane scheme to pump the groundwater from the Mojave to Orange County, the desert interior consists of unfenced national parks and national monuments, with no-unauthorized-entry military bases and massive blocks

of nearly untouched wilderness filling the map between the Sierra Nevada, Las Vegas, and the urban sprawl of Southern California.

Luckily for those who love this wild desert in its natural state, over the past hundred years a few visionaries were able to set aside much of this landscape as an immense desert preserve that rivals anything on Earth in size; only the vast Namibian desert preserve on the southwestern edge of the African continent is larger than the ten million protected acres of the Great Mojave Wilderness, from the tip of Death Valley National Park to San Gorgonio, within the new Sand to Snow National Monument.

Most Mojave visitors stay close to Joshua Tree National Park, and especially to its well-traveled sightseeing spots and tourist traps. If you get a flat tire or a dead battery on the Park Boulevard loop between Twentynine Palms and the unincorporated village of Joshua Tree, a friendly ranger will come along before long. And if your Airbnb turns out to be a lightly redecorated meth shack without a working toilet, you can always drive to a motel.

Get lost on a remote trail or break down off the highway and you're going to have a very different experience. Maybe you'll survive, and maybe you'll become part of our rich history of lost tourists. We add a few names to this roster every summer. If the names are known, anyway.

Maybe you're not ready to be on this list of people the Mojave chewed up and spit out. Maybe you have plans, plans that require coming home without the aid of a black vinyl body bag. The good news is that the Gospel of Desert Survival is short, simple, and easy to remember.

I. Water, and lots of it. Maybe you can dig up some sandy alkaline water from the damp edge of a wash, if you're lucky enough to be there just after a good soaking. Which is unlikely. Maybe you can build a "solar still" if you happen to drive around with science-project supplies. Or maybe you can bash open a barrel cactus, but it's best to leave that to the bighorn sheep, who don't get sick from the bitter mush within. Why not just carry plenty of water and not worry about your Eagle Scout technique? When you're at the grocery store buying whiskey and marshmallows for the campfire, fill up the extra space in the shopping cart with cheap plastic jugs of water. Ten dollars' worth of gallon-jug water in the trunk can significantly raise the odds of surviving your Mojave ordeal. (Please recycle the plastic jugs once you're rescued.)

II. Don't waste that phone charge! Of course you've got a car charger for your phone. Before a day hike or backcountry adventure, make sure that thing is charged up and don't run it down looking at Instagram or whatever. You're already in the scenic desert. While there are plenty of remote spots without any cell coverage, in much of the Mojave you can get a cell signal, even if you've got to walk up a hill first. Don't try this at high noon!

III. Don't walk in the heat of the day. If it's already hot when you start your day hike, it's going to be unbearable on the way back—especially at Amboy Crater, in Mojave Trails National Monument, where four day-hikers have perished since 2017. In the summer heat, dawn and dusk are the only times you want to be headed out for an easy walk. And if you're stuck with your car somewhere, it's best to stay put rather than walk into that inferno.

IV. A broken-down car is your friend. Your vehicle can be seen from a distance. It's bigger than you are, the glass and mirrors reflect light, and it's probably already on some kind of road or trail. Stay on the shady side when the sun's beating down.

V. Call for help before it's too late. When an Orange County couple got lost on a midday walk around Amboy Crater in August 2017, Kathie Barber managed to call 911. But Barber and her partner, Gen Miake, were already dead when the sheriff's helicopter found them.

VI. Watch where you step and where you reach. The best way to avoid a rattlesnake bite is to avoid stepping on a rattlesnake. To avoid black widow bites and scorpion stings, don't put your hands where you can't see. And leave those old army surplus snakebite kits at home; doctors say slicing up your flesh with a razor blade does far more harm than good. Just get to any desert hospital where antivenom is available.

VII. Flash floods kill. The most reliable way to die in the desert is to drive your car into floodwaters blocking a roadway. This is as deadly in downtown Palm Springs as in the Mojave Wilderness. And no matter how comfortable that shady wash looks on a hot summer day in monsoon season, remember that churning torrents of mud, boulders, dead cows, and floodwaters can come rolling down from dozens of miles away.

VIII. Check the condition of your car, your rental RV, whatever you're relying on to get you back to civilization. Make sure your tires are evenly inflated and have enough tread for a road trip. Is your spare tire functional? Enough coolant in the reservoir? How about engine oil? And don't forget the full tank of gas! Service stations are few and far between.

IX. Tell someone who cares. Heading off to the desert wilds? Text the people who care whether you live or die. And tell the desk staff at your hotel, or your vacation-rental host, or the rangers at your campground. Sign the trail registers. Leave a note on the dashboard if you're heading away from your vehicle. The more clues for rescuers, the more likely they'll find you while you're still breathing.

X. Don't go rock climbing alone. Crawling up boulders has become a popular pastime, despite the well-established effects of gravity and routine deaths and critical injuries from falls. In May 2018, the New Zealander Claire Nelson fell fifteen feet from a boulder in Joshua Tree National Park and spent four terrifying days on the ground with a shattered hip before rescuers went looking for her. If you must try rock climbing, do so with a buddy.

XI. But choose your buddy carefully. In the sweltering summer of 2017, twenty-year-old Rachel Nguyen went to Joshua Tree to celebrate her birthday with her ex-boyfriend Joseph Orbeso, twenty-one. Just two miles from the Maze Loop parking lot, where their vehicle was found, Orbeso shot his ex through the skull with his .40-caliber semiautomatic pistol, which he carried loaded on a short day hike in a national park. Then he turned the gun on himself.

XII. And finally, if all else fails and your time is at hand, know that most people relax at the end. Find a place to sit down, in the shade, if there's any shade. None of us live forever. And not enough of us get the time to sit alone in the quiet wilderness and contemplate our own existence and our place in the world.

THE KNOWN UNKNOWN: TALES OF YUCCA MAN

The story you'll hear most often goes like this: There's a young marine on guard duty in some far-off corner of the massive Twentynine Palms desert training base. He hears an awful sound in the dark, something like a growl. Then, the breathing, coming from one side of his lonesome little guard booth and now from the other.

It's circling him.

He steps out into the dark, his sidearm drawn. There it stands: eight feet tall, an unbearable stench, the eyes glowing like red coals.

Sometimes, the marine is knocked unconscious by the shaggy-haired beast and found hours later by the next shift. One version occurs at the old rifle range, where the watchman—also armed, with a rifle—wakes from the assault to find his weapon bent in half.

Since the 1970s, when the Mojave Desert base expanded from a primitive World War II encampment, there have been regular reports of new recruits terrorized by both the Yucca Man and pranksters inspired by the tales. But most sightings of the spectral creature come from campers and hikers at Joshua Tree National Park. Tents have been opened in the night by stinking monstrosities, and there is an occasional large footprint or blurry photograph submitted as evidence. A snapshot from the Hidden Valley campground has made the rounds for a decade now; the figure bounding over the boulders looks much like the iconic Bigfoot from the Patterson-Gimlin film of 1967.

Since the 1960s, when tales of Yucca Man and his desert cohorts were commonly reported by Southern California newspapers and television stations, amateur "cryptozoologists" and Bigfoot researchers have analyzed the blurry pictures and measured the prints in the sand, all in the effort to document a flesh-and-blood creature they believe exists alongside everyday mammals such as bears, coyotes, and humans.

But the Indians who lived in California long before European colonization considered these creatures to be supernatural entities, with names that often translated to "hairy devils." The people took care to avoid the gloomy spots where the devils were often seen.

The Tongva living around the Santa Ana River called the devils' hideout east of the river's source in the San Bernardino Mountains the "Camp of the Takwis," pronounced like "Tahquitz," the desert monster known to the Cahuilla of Agua Caliente.

According to John Reed Swanton's *The Indian*

Tribes of North America, "Takwis" also survives as a site name at the head of the Santa Margarita River, at Temecula Creek. Throughout Palm Springs and the Coachella Valley, you'll see it spelled "Tahquitz"—the angry specter's unhappy home in the region is the cursed Tahquitz Canyon, just off Highway 111 in Palm Springs.

Sometimes the Takwis or Tahquitz played a role in creation stories, as in Cahuilla culture. Other times the creature was an omen, or simply something weird in the wilderness that should be avoided. To the Cahuilla, the Tahquitz could be the "original shaman" and a murderous monstrosity that collected victims from Tahquitz Rock (also known as Lily Rock). "Tahquitz has also been said to manifest as a large green fireball moving through the night sky," according to the *Weird California* travel guide.

That coastal and desert Indians should know the same creature is not in itself cause for skepticism: Under various names and dressed in myriad traditions, Yucca Man has been reported in the wilder parts of Southern California as long as people have lived here.

In Fontana, that hard and windblown Inland Empire town, there was a famed racetrack north of Foothill Boulevard called Mickey Thompson's Fontana Dragway. From 1955 until the dragway's closure in 1972, following a series of gruesome fatalities on the track, spectators repeatedly saw something they called the Speedway Monster.

Assumed to be a "wild man" native to the foothills of the nearby San Bernardino Mountains, it had the habit of crossing the rural land at the dragway's edge during car races that produced horrific noise and violence.

In the new suburbs of Antelope Valley, encounters with the Mojave Sasquatch reached epidemic levels from the late 1960s through late 1970s, as new housing developments in Lancaster and Palmdale pushed into the wild desert and secret technology was tested at Edwards Air Force Base and Lockheed's notorious Skunk Works facility.

The *Antelope Valley Daily Ledger-Gazette* described the common features of the eyewitness reports in a staff report from June 1973, beneath the headline "Bigfoot Surfaces Again in Palmdale, Nine-Mile Canyon." According to the reporter Chuck Wheeler, "the creature likes to run around houses, leaving footprints. That is its M.O. in the East Lancaster area where footprints were found around several houses recently. One woman reported that the creature ran around her house and scratched at the door. A small boy sent to tell his father supper was ready was found hours later crying near the corral. When asked what happened to him, he answered that a big, furry man would not let him pass."

Southern California encounters were common enough in the 1970s to keep multiple Bigfoot-investigation groups busy taking reports. In March 1973, a babysitter and three marines—separately, we presume—reported seeing the Sasquatch in Lancaster. Nerves were frayed to the point that two separate vigilante groups searching for the monster nearly killed each other, according to the files of the Bigfoot Field Researchers Organization: "In May 1973, a search party in Lancaster attempting to follow up on several 'Big Foot' reports was forced to take cover when another party on the same sort of search panicked and started shooting when they thought they were being approached by a large creature. Fortunately, no one was injured."

In recent years, the hair-covered, red-eyed "Sierra Highway Devil" has been repeatedly spotted by terrified drivers on Highway 14 near the junction with Pearblossom Highway, sometimes just before dawn, always running along or across the road.

The strangest tales come from Edwards AFB itself. The desert base adjoins the massive Rogers Dry Lake, with its miles of smooth desert runways, and is famed for its "Right Stuff" test pilots and landings of NASA's space shuttles. There is significant subterranean infrastructure at Edwards, with the personnel and technology required to keep secret aircraft a secret. Security cameras were always pointed at sensitive areas. According to persistent stories from Edwards, those cameras repeatedly captured images of Desert Sasquatch moving through the tunnels by night. Entire families of the hairy monsters apparently traveled the base's buildings and corridors, appearing and disappearing at will, to the bewilderment of base police sent chasing after the phantasms.

With the report of Sergeant Michael House, a base policeman, a rare real name is attached to an Edwards encounter with something known to air force security forces as "Blue Eyes."

Bobbie Ann Slate, a tireless Bigfoot researcher, collected this report from the base policeman who was patrolling the old "sled track" section of the base, where the notorious Thelemite wizard and Jet Propulsion Laboratory cofounder Jack Parsons tried out his rockets, and where Nazi V-2s had once been tested on a specially built railroad:

> Heading back to the main base, I noticed maybe 200–300 yards to my left, these large blue eyes. I do a lot of night hunting and it was strange—they were larger than anything I'd ever seen before. The [blue eyes] had to be about four inches apart and seven feet off the ground. I stopped the truck and sat there watching them. It was too dark to see any body shape to the thing. The blue glows proceeded toward my truck at a right angle for about 100 yards and then stopped.

As an overpowering stench filled the desert air, Sergeant House saw the huge blue eyes again, now just fifty yards away. "The movement of the eyes was extremely fast. Another thing that bothered me was that they didn't bob up and down. It was like two lights on a wire moving from one point to another." A radio call gave him a good reason to drive away fast.

Because of the ribbing he suffered after filing a report, others in the squadron refrained from making formal statements about their encounters.

But the encounters didn't end. Not until 2009 would Edwards Air Force Base officially acknowledge the many incidents with Blue Eyes and other strange phenomena.

According to a 2009 article in the base newsletter, *Inside Edwards*, the entity known as Blue Eyes was much discussed at a reunion of the 6510th Air Police Squadron officers who worked on base between 1973 and 1979, known as the 6510th Desert Rats. Lisa Camplin, of the 95th Security Forces Squadron, published several such recollections for the official Edwards newsletter:

"Attendees traded memories of their bizarre experiences on patrol such as seeing 'Blue Eyes,' the local version of a Yeti near South Base or 'Marvin of the Mojave,' a ghost who could be heard but not seen and who left size-10 sneaker imprints in the sand."

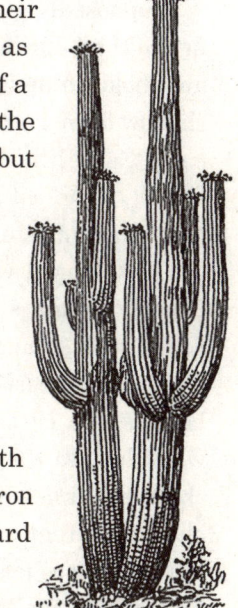

The now-retired Edwards guards also recalled "observing unexplainable objects in the skies [and] seeing disappearing tail lights on the dry lake beds."

The Desert Rats' motto, shared with the Air Force Test Center the squadron served, was *Ad Inexplorata*, or "Toward the Unknown."

As with the padres' old stories of

"hairy monsters" living along the Santa Ana and Santa Margarita Rivers, written accounts of monsters in the Antelope Valley date back to the Spanish colonial era. Horace Bell, famed for his role in the frontier vigilante group called the Los Angeles Rangers, later wrote two influential books about life in mid-nineteenth-century California. One of those, *On the Old West Coast: Being Further Reminiscences of a Ranger*, tells of a shadowy winged beast at Elizabeth Lake, that deep-water hole where the Sierra Pelona Mountains meet Antelope Valley. The "sag pond" was created by the San Andreas Fault, and successive generations have branded this generally welcome geographic feature—ample fresh water in the desert!—as a cursed place.

Supposedly given its old Spanish name by no less a figure than Junípero Serra himself, the Laguna del Diablo held an awful creature, a beast that would fly in shadow form over the rancho from the 1830s—when the early California legislator Don Pedro Carrillo (grandfather of the actor Leo Carrillo) abandoned the place following a mysterious fire and general bad feelings.

The winged wraith flew over the hacienda of Don Chico Vasquez, a man unimpressed by the folklore surrounding the lake. It was his foremen who alerted the Don to the beast thrashing in the mud on the cursed lake's shore. He saw it, too, but the creature vanished—whether into the lake or into the sky or into thin air, they never knew. Cattle and horses began disappearing shortly thereafter, with the eventual discovery of several carcasses leading to the belief that the devil in the lake had grown hungry for meat.

As with the "hairy monsters," the winged beast of the lake also assaulted the rancho with its vile stench.

Don Chico Vasquez had had enough and sold cheap to Miguel Leonis, the famed Big Basque and King of Calabasas. Leonis not only proposed to capture the lake monster that had bedeviled his Indian, Spanish, and American predecessors but also planned to make money on the deal. The Big Basque contracted with the Sells Brothers Circus, which operated across the country from its base in Columbus, Ohio, from 1862 to 1895. According to *On the Old West Coast*, Leonis's contract with the Sells Brothers would have made him significantly richer had the flying lake beast been captured: "That if the python is such as the party of the first part describes it to be, and if the party of the first part succeeds in taking it alive, then the party of the second part agrees to pay the party of the first part the sum of $20,000."

Instead, the winged snake flew east after being shot by the Big Basque's hunting party. According to legend, this was the same "dragon" killed outside Tombstone, Arizona, in 1890. But evidence of the monstrosity's corpse has proved elusive, and Elizabeth Lake remains deeply haunted to this day.

While Yucca Man and its cohorts are often described as huge, hair-covered humanoids, there are nearly as many reports of shadow beasts lacking any real definition beyond their brilliant glowing eyes—often red, sometimes blue, as in the Edwards AFB reports. Such brazenly paranormal entities have much in common with England's Owlman and West Virginia's Mothman—or the Mojave Desert's own Cement Monster.

Anyone who has taken the scenic drive on Highway 18 from the West Mojave up to Big Bear Lake has driven past the huge concrete mine eating into the mountainside and national forest. Now owned by the Mitsubishi Cement Corporation and surrounded by security fencing, there was a time when many of its graded roads could be easily accessed from the two-lane highway.

In March 1988, two U.S. marines returning from a day of snow skiing at Big Bear encountered the red-eyed shadow giant and pursued it into the strip mine. One of them, Ken Fox, sent his report of the incident to the Sasquatch researcher Douglas E. Trapp in Texas.

"From the left side of the road something very large seemed to stand up on two legs and run across the road," Fox wrote. "The bottom half looked human, covered with hair. The top half wasn't very visible, but appeared monsterish, scary in other words. The headlights only got the bottom half, and the damn thing ran out about 150 feet in front of us. It made it across the road in three strides. I distinctively remember seeing the arms pumping back and forth just like any of us would do if sprinting across the road in front of a car. It appeared to be 8 feet tall."

What was it? Ken Fox's buddy recognized it immediately: "It's the Cement Monster! After him!"

They briefly pursued but, having no luck, continued back to base at Twentynine Palms. If the cement mine is still haunted by this monster, it is considerably more difficult for people to access the cuts in the mountainside today.

This transition zone between the transverse mountain ranges and the High Desert is rich with reports of similar monsters, from the beast seen as recently as 2012 at Devil's Punchbowl to the Sasquatch stalking hikers at Big Rock Canyon.

Yucca Man, too, is connected to these immense mountains via the Little San Bernardino ranges from Joshua Tree National Park westward into Sand to Snow National Monument up to San Gorgonio and Barton Flats, where generations of summer-camp kids have suffered sleepless nights after hearing campfire tales of a diabolic forest monster lurking just beyond the cabins.

The harsh, hot badlands that comprise much of Anza-Borrego Desert State Park are home to many strange and terrible stories of the creature that has been called the "Missing Link" and the "Borrego Sandman." The Sandman has been seen by twentieth-century gold hunters and rock hounds, and is most often described as being an enormous primate with whitish fur and glowing red eyes.

This Missing Link of Deadman's Hole is reportedly a mass murderer.

Once the gold rush reached Southern California's mountains and deserts, in the later 1800s, prospectors and bandits quickly made the area home. Discoveries of gold at Julian and in the badlands to the east brought many hopeful miners to the scorching San Diego County desert, along with many stagecoaches loaded with suspicious characters. One of them, Peg Leg Smith, claimed to have found and then lost a "mine" near the Salton Sea where gold nuggets could be picked up off the ground. And a couple of characters from Julian, Edward Dean and Charles Cox, claimed to have shot a Sasquatch dead.

An 1888 article in *The San Diego Union* reported that the men had found and then killed the monster at Deadman's Hole, northeast of Warner Ranch. Delivery of the mysterious creature's corpse was promised, but it never appeared in San Diego. More than a century later, a *Daily Transcript* reporter named Herbert Lockwood went digging for the old story and found it in an issue dated April 1 of that year.

A more credible report was published in the same newspaper a dozen years earlier, in March 1876. A man named Turner Helm claimed he saw a "missing link" near Warner Ranch (four miles south of present-day Warner Springs). Described as a bearlike giant with a human face, the report generated great interest because of the many unsolved murders at nearby Deadman's Hole, then a water stop on the Butterfield stage line.

The bodies had been piling up at the stagecoach stop's water hole for two decades, with the victims including a French-Basque shepherd, several dubious individuals on the run from the law or creditors, and a wealthy San Franciscan named William Blair.

Many of the victims were found with bruised and broken necks, their money or gold untouched. The last unsolved murder at the water hole dates to 1922, when another strangled victim was found there, sixty-four years after the first recorded murders at the hole.

Deadman's Hole—"Deadman Hole" on modern maps—is located in a grove of live oaks about fifteen yards east of California State Highway 79, an eight-mile drive from today's Warner Springs, just southeast of the place called Takwi, at the headwaters of the Santa Margarita River.

The visitor to the Deadman's Hole of today should look for the small, plainly lettered sign that reads "U.S. Navy Remote Training Area," at an unmarked crossroads just before Sunshine Summit. As at Edwards and Twentynine Palms, here the marines train side by side with the elusive Sasquatch of Southern California's wild lands.

THE BOY WHO VANISHED

San Gorgonio stands 11,503 feet tall, the highest peak in Southern California, the snow-capped mountain that looms over Yucca Valley. It's part of Sand to Snow National Monument now, part of a chain of protected wilderness and protected natural landscapes stretching across the Mojave, hundreds of miles into Death Valley and into the White Mountains and beyond.

A herd of desert bighorn or mule deer—or the mountain lions that follow—could wander for six hundred miles from Mount San Gorgonio down to Big Morongo Canyon, across the Little San Bernardino Mountains, eastward through Joshua Tree National Park, north over the Sheephole Valley Wilderness, and across Mojave Trails National Monument, through Mojave National Preserve, up the spine of the Panamints.

In theory, anyway. Once the wildlife crossings are built over Highway 62 and Interstate 40 and Interstate 15. Hopefully soon.

Nearly three decades ago, a troop of Boy Scouts was hiking up to the top of San Gorgonio. Jared Negrete was in this troop, an eighth grader from El Monte nearing his thirteenth birthday. Hundreds of people do this hike every summer, when temperatures are comfortable at the summit. But like most mountains, that last thousand feet is hard, especially if you've never done such a thing before.

Jared Negrete was exhausted. The troop leader, inexplicably, left this twelve-year-old boy alone to wait on the trail. The rest of the Boy Scouts continued to the peak with the lone adult in the group.

When they returned, on the way down, Jared wasn't there.

It was July 19, 1991. The hike began at Camp Tahquitz, in the forest south of Big Bear, a place where generations of kids have spent memorable weeks at summer camp. Who leaves a child on a mountainside? The expectation is that the adult chaperone will bring the Boy Scouts home.

Search-and-rescue teams from the Marine Corps base in Twentynine Palms and the San Bernardino Sheriff's Department scoured the mountain for nineteen days.

They found his canteen, his beef jerky, wrappers from candy, some footprints that matched his shoes. They also found his pocket camera.

A dozen pictures had been shot, and when the film was developed it was established that eleven of the photographs were taken before Jared got lost. They were landscapes, pictures of the forest and the wild mountainside in summertime.

The twelfth picture was of Jared Negrete himself—a selfie, in the current vernacular. Because his face is illuminated by the automatic camera's flash, the search teams decided this one was taken the night he was lost to the world.

Only his eyes and nose appear in the photo. Even without the emotional clue of the mouth, the picture is heavy with dread. His eyes are haunted by dire circumstance. It is the last glimpse of a boy who was never seen again.

His remains were never found. No bones, no shred of clothing, no shoes. Temperatures were mild throughout the nineteen-day search, and there was plenty of water running down the mountain in creeks and streams.

This young boy, on a hike up a Southern California mountain surrounded on all sides by roads and civilization, just vanished.

RAVENS

On an evening walk through Onaga Valley a week or so back, I saw this pair of ravens, the same ravens I've seen for years and years in this one particular place. They've raised several rounds of children, who then grow up and move away and still come to visit and argue every now and then, but day to day it's just this pair, in their place. You'll see them on a Joshua tree at sunrise, talking it over, watching that yellow ball of fire rising over the boulders. You'll see them in the afternoons, buzzing the coyotes or my dog, or cackling at a mountain bicyclist racing by, but until this moment I had never seen their home.

They live in a small cave about a hundred feet over the valley, in a wall of rock, facing north so it's shady and cooler during our long summer, and I got the feeling they were embarrassed that the human who so often walks these trails had finally spotted their secret lair. After all, anyone who regularly talks back to the ravens in some sad approximation of raven calls is not someone who should be able to spot their home, even after a decade or so of looking for it.

But there it was, with all kinds of junk on the rock ledge, things they'd found, mostly sticks of some kind. A real desert homestead. They rushed inside and, I'm certain, hoped I wouldn't remember. And sure enough, now I can't quite spot the small shadow on the rock wall where the ravens have made their home.

What do we know about ravens? More all the time, but they remain mysterious.

In the wild, ravens can live for decades. Domesticated ravens have lived for forty-five years.

While a flock of crows is called a "murder," some colorful terms for groups of ravens include an "unkindness" and a "conspiracy." But you don't need to get clever about it; just call them ravens.

The raven is the largest and heaviest of the corvids, and the bird we call the common raven is found all over the northern hemisphere. They'll eat about anything and they don't mind working for it: Ravens use tools, like humans. They'll use sticks or wire or rocks to get food, break shells, hide food from other animals. And once they figure out something clever, they like to teach the other ravens about the discovery, like dropping hard-shelled nuts on a road so that passing cars will break the shells for them.

Ravens are masters of deception. They'll act like they're storing food in one place, but then they'll casually drop it somewhere else.

The Book of Genesis tells the story of Noah trusting a raven to find land after the great flood. "And he sent forth a raven, which went forth to and fro, until the waters were dried up from off the earth." Why Genesis then tries to get us to believe Noah sent out a simple-minded dove to do the same thing is one of those many Bible mysteries.

The Norse god Odin traveled with a pair of ravens named Thought and Memory. They brought him news from around the world—which makes sense, because ravens have a rich and complex language. And like human language, raven language varies from place to place. The ravens in my chunk of the desert will pronounce things differently from the ravens in Stovepipe Wells or Lee's Ferry.

DOC SPRINGER'S LAST WORD IN HEALTH: ZZYZX

"Hello folks! This is your old friend Curtis Springer, coming to you direct from our beautiful new studios located at Zzyzx Community Church, on the shores of beautiful Lake Tuendae. And as founder and pastor of our church, I want to invite you and your loved ones to come worship with us. Come with or without money, and spend a day or a week or a lifetime, as you care to, and enjoy our beautiful twelve-thousand-acre estate that belongs to God. We have no promotion, no real estate for sale. Just come on out here and enjoy our wonderful hot mineral water baths, the finest of foods in abundance, our wonderful desert-pure fresh air—no smog, no fog. Come and learn to breathe again! Lay out in the sunshine. Oh, you'll love it here. You'll get a greater joy out of life. So until the same time tomorrow, over the same wonderful radio station, I'll say bye-bye, and God bless you all."

—**THE REVEREND DR. CURTIS SPRINGER, KMTR 570 AM, 1944**

Only a few miles south of Interstate 15, with its numbing traffic of Las Vegas tourists and long-haul truckers, there is an oasis out of a Hollywood-Sahara dream. It sits at the end of a gravelly road that winds around glossy brown volcanic rock piles, as the sandy earth gives way to saltbush and marshland, thick with tall green reeds, busy with dragonflies and visiting shorebirds.

This is Soda Springs, where mineral waters are forced from the underworld at the western edge of a vast dry lakebed that meets the jagged mountain ranges of Mojave National Preserve. Out of this wild panorama rise neat rows of palm trees—enormous California and Mexican fan palms, with seven decades' worth of dead fronds reaching to the ground. The palm-lined driveway leads to a small village from another time.

This boulevard is divided by a wide sandy median with more trees, an old nesting box on a pole, and park benches facing the small lake ringed by willows. The coots have the run of the pond: a half dozen of the black-feathered creatures glide across the water.

On a steamy, still day, as the season's last monsoon thunderstorms cook up over the eastern mountains, there is shade from the overgrown smoke trees, but not much relief from the 104-degree heat. The village consists of a handful of white plaster buildings along the grandly named Boulevard of Dreams. Rows of dorm-style guest rooms are across the way, with small, shared patios between them. The grandest building has an outdoor dining room with the whole Eastern Mojave for a backdrop, along with a crescent of those giant Mexican palm trees framing the immense scenery.

Just below the pond's surface, small carp dart around: Mohave tui chub, the last pure specimens, accidentally saved from extinction or crossbreeding by a curious character who introduced the rare fish from a nearby spring—what had been their last refuge—when he built his charming little acre-and-a-half lake.

The most stunning parts of the Mojave Desert, both natural and man-made, are nearly always empty of people.

For thirty years, from 1944 to 1974, a self-appointed doctor of medicine and theology lived out here, presiding over his busy, arid empire of health potions and faith. He was "the Reverend" Curtis Springer, "Doc Springer" to his friends, and anybody who mailed an envelope of cash to the world-famous Zzyzx Mineral Springs was indeed his blessed friend.

To build his Moroccan-inspired oasis Springer bused in the winos from "the Nickel"—Skid Row, in downtown Los Angeles. They got three meals a day and a bunk for their troubles, but most headed back to Fifth Street once they figured out that alcohol wasn't part of Doc Springer's menu.

When his hotel, cross-shaped soaking pool, and radio studio were completed, Springer broadcast his invitation to anyone with the means to travel out to Soda Springs and take his many cures. Generous donations were expected. To those who couldn't afford a visit to his enchanting resort in the desert but still enjoyed his sermons, carried by more than three hundred radio stations, he offered mail-order cures both commonsensical and absurd—it's hard to argue with carrot juice and mineral baths, but his "Mo-Hair" baldness cure required the rubbing of Soda Lake salts upon one's scalp while hanging upside down and holding one's breath.

The quack complaints eventually made their way to the Law in the late 1960s, after Springer had plied his weird trade for a quarter century. In 1969, while another Mojave mystic prepared to bring his Family back from Death Valley to Hollywood, Doc Springer went on trial for selling bogus medicine. He served only forty-nine days for his fraud conviction, but his troubles weren't over. The Bureau of Land Management demanded he dismantle the resort: He held nothing but a mining claim on the twelve thousand acres, and he was selling Zzyzx Springs residential lots to his loyalists.

But why "Zzyzx"? It was the last word in the English language, Springer claimed, so it was the last word in health.

Doc Springer was forced off his oasis in 1974, and he died in Las Vegas a dozen years later. He was an old-time country con man who never really hurt anybody and provided some hope and adventure for bored, gullible Americans staring at their radio in the night.

Today, Zzyzx is the Desert Studies Center, part of Cal State Fullerton and home to UC Riverside's occasional extended-education outings for the peculiar few who want to spend a long weekend learning about rocks and bugs and other desert delights.

Drive slowly, should you visit. The bighorn sheep enjoy the water and wetland, too, and can often be seen at dawn or dusk.

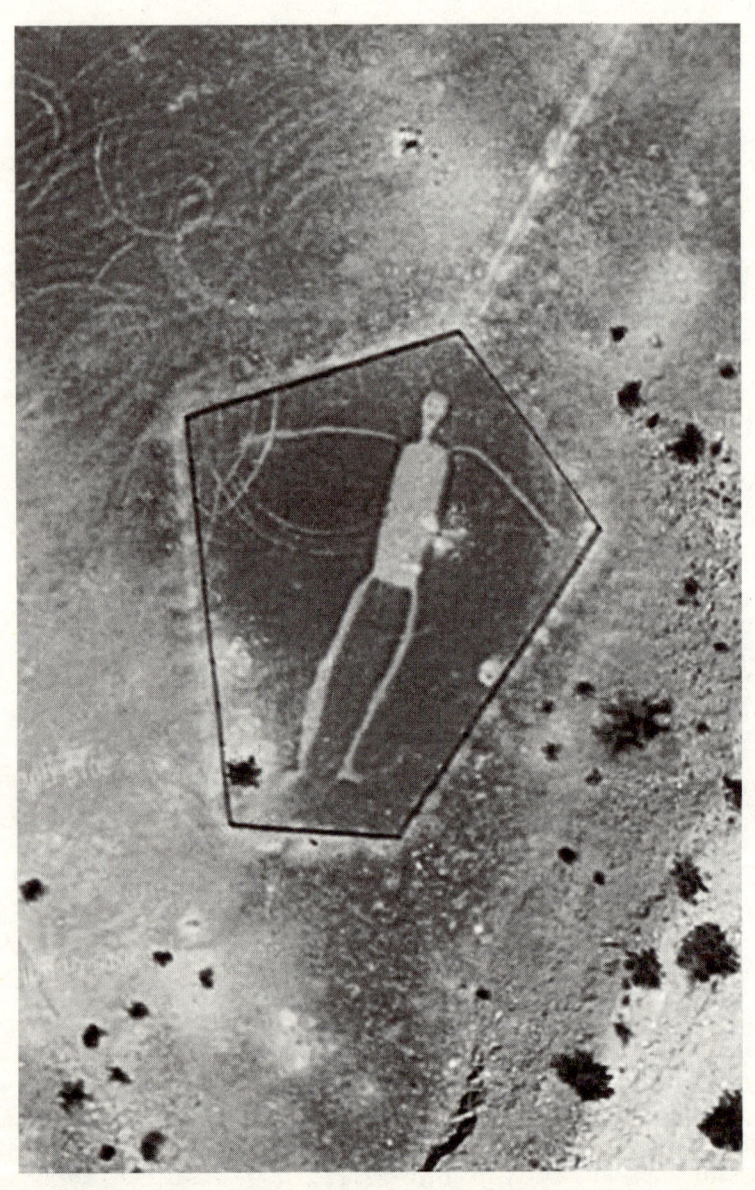

HORROR OF THE SOLAR LODGE

Between Blythe and Needles on U.S. 95, you'll find a desert outpost called Vidal, just north of the San Bernardino–Riverside county line. If you take Highway 62 out of Joshua Tree all the way to the Colorado River, when you cross Highway 95 you're in Vidal Junction, where you'll find a gas station or two and one of those California Agricultural Inspection Stations, where they ask you if you're bringing any vegetables from Arizona or wherever, if you're coming from the east.

Now, if you head south on U.S. 95 a few miles, then right past the railroad tracks, you'll see a dirt street, Old Parker Road, and just a few lots to the east you'll find a neat little white-and-blue house with a shady porch and an interesting historical marker outside, put up by E Clampus Vitus, as per usual.

The marker explains that this was the home of Wyatt Earp, legendary lawman and gunslinger and gambler of the Old West, and his third wife, Josephine Sarah, known as Sadie. It was the only permanent home they owned, from 1925 to 1928. The Earps had the house moved down from its original location up the highway in Calzona, where it was the only surviving building after the rest of Calzona burnt to the ground.

Wyatt Earp died at age eighty at his rented house in Los Angeles early in 1929, the year the Great Depression began. Because Sadie was Jewish and had a cemetery plot up in Colma, the City of the Dead, she buried his cremated remains there and joined him in 1944.

Wyatt Earp spent a lot of time in Los Angeles with cowboy actors and horseback stunt riders, Tom Mix and Douglas Fairbanks. He knew everybody. He spent time in Alaska with his friend Jack London, and was frequently invited to the movie sets run by his friend John Ford. But for whatever reason, this living legend of the Old West could not get a movie deal, could not sell his story. Besides, he was still active, still mining his Happy Days claim outside of Vidal, where, if you look real close, you can see the speck of a settlement named for him: Earp, California, where he built a rough cabin.

He was a deputy sheriff of San Bernardino County, too. Honorary deputy, at least. And in the 1910s he did a lot of freelance work for the Los Angeles police. A bounty hunter. He is remembered for capably capturing various wanted men in Mexico and beyond. He got involved with a mining war up around Trona, and wherever he went, people would argue with him about his handling of the O.K. Corral shootout, which he defended. People would complain about various famous boxing matches he had refereed, too. Mostly they just wanted to talk to a legend.

In the Depression years, after Wyatt Earp passed on, Vidal and his namesake village of Earp became part of a busy and violent labor camp, where thousands of men labored on public-works projects such as the aqueduct and the highways, and saloons and package-liquor stores lined the roads. The Wobblies, the Industrial Workers of the World, came to town in great numbers, and you can imagine Wyatt Earp would've enjoyed seeing his quiet desert home as part of yet another western boomtown, with all the drinking and gambling and fighting that came with it.

But the quiet times returned to this hot, flat corner of the desert, until the 1960s. That's when an outlaw branch of Aleister Crowley's O.T.O. lodge took up residence. O.T.O. stands for *Ordo Templi Orientis*, a sort of Rosicrucian-Masonic occult organization that originated in Austria around 1905—the same year the Wobblies formed, for what it's worth.

Crowley was a wanderer, a mountaineer, and a poet, born a little too late for the Romantic era, the time of William Blake and Mary Shelley. In 1910 he took charge of O.T.O. in the British Isles and made the organization his own. Crowley was fond of attention and loved ceremony. This order of the Eastern Templars never involved more than a few hundred people, and often no more than a few dozen, but they were often the people who left a mark upon the world.

The California chapter, the Agape Lodge, was based in Pasadena. They performed the Gnostic Mass, based on the beautiful ceremony of the Eastern Orthodox Church, which Crowley enjoyed while traveling in Russia. And they had some interesting members there in Pasadena, people you've heard about before: L. Ron Hubbard, and the Jet Propulsion Lab cofounder Jack Parsons, and Marjorie Cameron. Jack Parsons was corresponding with Crowley in 1946, when Parsons and Hubbard were performing their great desert ritual, the Babalon Working. Crowley warned Parsons to be careful with this stuff, even as Crowley made no secret of his distaste for Parsons and Hubbard and the whole Pasadena crew. Still, Parsons was into something heavy.

Aleister Crowley had appointed himself prophet of the new age. He spoke at length to an entity that looks just like our mythological big-headed gray aliens, and that entity dictated a book to Crowley, in Egypt, *The Book of the Law*. Crowley said he would usher in the Aeon of Horus.

But Jack Parsons, this vulgar American working in his Southern California garage, was the one who would usher in the Space Age. And in that Babalon Working, it is said, something dropped into our reality, something we have never been able to send back. Crowley himself was dead a few months later. And by 1952 Parsons was dead, too. Blown to bits in an explosion.

The Agape Lodge, the only O.T.O. lodge remaining after World War II, had been housed in those years within Jack Parsons's mansion at 1003 South Orange

Avenue. At its peak, the house was filled with artists and bohemians and people on the very edge of science, people such as Robert Cornog, one of the handful of Manhattan Project physicists who unleashed the atomic bomb. He lived there and was a dear friend of Jack Parsons. The Agape Lodge faded when Parsons had to sell the big Craftsman house—L. Ron Hubbard had run away with all of Parsons's money. For a decade, the O.T.O. was quiet.

This is why, beginning in 1962, a member of that Pasadena lodge named Ray Burlingame began to initiate new members, forming the outlaw O.T.O. congregation he called the Solar Lodge. Ritual magick was back in California, just in time for the Age of Aquarius.

Within a few years, this new organization, this illegal spawn of Crowley's A∴A∴, Astrum Argenteum, was very visible in both Los Angeles and the deserts to the east. Right there across the street from the University of Southern California, the Solar Lodge operated a magick bookstore called the Eye of Horus. It's where you could buy all kinds of rare books about ceremonial

magick, especially books by Aleister Crowley. Los Angeles had the best occult bookstores, then and now, and while Led Zeppelin's Jimmy Page is an Englishman, like his hero Crowley, Page bought his Crowley books in Los Angeles. A book called *Trampled Under Foot*, by Barney Hoskyns, reveals that Page was a collector rather than a scholar of the stuff. Showing off his occult collection to a guest who knew Hebrew, Page was deeply rattled when this guest began reading aloud from a rare magick book. Page apparently had no idea the mysterious symbols were part of a language spoken by millions.

Well, the Solar Lodge had the good stuff, the rare stuff: letters and drawings and charts. And as the lodge expanded, it purchased some desert property for monthlong rituals in the middle of nowhere. In the few years between its official founding in 1965 and the events of 1969, the lodge bought up real estate in and around Vidal, California. It owned and operated the gas station, an Atlantic Richfield franchise, and the motel and the restaurant and the bar. It had another Eye of Horus bookstore, in Blythe. It had all kinds of people out there working for nothing in the desert sun, seekers and searchers, lost souls. And it had a storage building that contained the rarest of Crowley papers and books. Here in the desert, far from prying eyes, the members of the Solar Lodge were building their ark, their Ark of the Covenant.

It was this building that a six-year-old child named Anthony Saul Gibbons accidentally set on fire. The initiates were furious. So they tortured the child by burning his fingers with matches, and then they chained him inside a six-foot-square shipping crate, with buckets for water, for food, for human waste. When the sheriff's deputies arrived on July 26, 1969, the boy had reportedly been locked inside for fifty-six days. His mother and father were members of the Solar Lodge.

This outrage became known as the Boy in the Box. Some of the adults fled, others faced trial; there were felony convictions, and there were charges dismissed. Because they did not look like hippies and some of them had professional jobs in Los Angeles, the scandal of the Boy in the Box was not immediately seen to be a story of an occult lodge. It was instead called a commune by the newspapers, at least until the trial in October 1969, in Indio, when the occult angle became better known. There were many children at the compound, generally kept away from their parents, instructed in dark arts, and spoken to in "very severe tones." The Solar Lodge teachers were fond of physical punishment. Also in October 1969, Charles Manson and a dozen members of his murderous Family were arrested at Barker

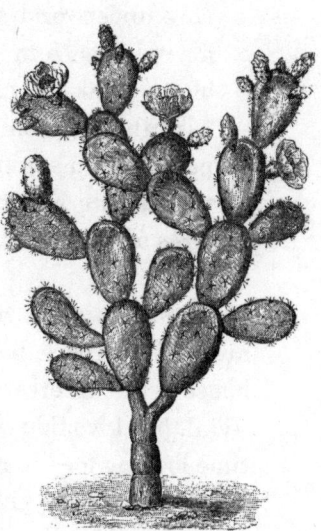

Ranch, on the west slope of Death Valley's Panamint Mountains.

Manson was hiding out after the murders in Los Angeles he'd orchestrated. He had a strange philosophy. According to past members of the Solar Lodge, he borrowed his desert-compound apocalyptic race war idea from the Solar Lodge itself. He was not an official member, but he hung around just enough to get what he needed.

Here's how Alex Constantine described the cult in his 1996 book *Ordis Templis Intelligentis*:

> The group subscribed to a grim, apocalyptic view of the world precipitated by race wars, and the prophecy made a lasting impression on Charles Manson, who passed through the lodge. In the L.A. underworld, the O.T.O. spin-off was known for indulgence in sadomasochism, drug dealing, blood drinking, child molestation and murder. Like the Manson Family, they used drugs, sex, psycho-drama and fear to tear down the mind of the initiate and rebuild it according to the desires of the cult's inner-circle.

The remains of the Solar Lodge desert compound are still out there, baking in the sun. The Wyatt Earp house is an interesting stop while traveling through Vidal, but I would recommend you not spend too much time looking for the remnants of this occult compound. Crowley had been given the sensational nickname "the Wickedest Man in the World" by the magazine *John*

Bull, but his oft-stated philosophy was that "every man and woman is a star." The Solar Lodge may have deified Crowley, but they missed his point. They were not magicians seeking the light of the world. They were just plain evil.

EULOGY FOR A SPACE MISSION

At the Goldstone Deep Space Observatory, located in a lonesome and quiet bowl in the mountains midway between Barstow and Badwater, there was some sadness in the early hours of September 15, 2017, but also pride and joy, because one of the greatest space-science missions in our brief history of exploring the solar system came to an end at 4:55 a.m. Mojave Time. That's when contact was lost with the *Cassini* spacecraft as it plunged, as planned, into the churning atmosphere of Saturn. "The Grand Finale," it was called.

Goldstone is one of three deep-space antenna stations spread around our planet, placed 120 degrees apart. As the world turns, the signal from *Cassini* passed over from one antenna station to the next: one set in the quiet open space here in the California desert, one west of Madrid, and one southwest of the Australian capital, Canberra. These isolated antenna complexes take in a steady stream of transmissions from our far-flung robotic correspondents, including the *Voyager* probes, the *Mars Express* and *Mars Odyssey*, and

Cassini, whose retirement ended a mission that began twenty years earlier, with its launch in 1997.

Cassini reached Saturn in 2004 and spent nine years in close company with the ringed planet and its many strange moons: moons with plumes of water and snow, and lakes of liquid methane. There may well be life on these moons, especially in the water seas beneath rocky crust. To protect those biospheres, *Cassini* was deliberately piloted into Saturn itself, burning up so that it would not infect these mysterious moons.

The final signal was heard not at Goldstone—which was turning toward the sun with the rest of the California desert by then—but at NASA's Deep Space Network antenna complex in Canberra, which was facing mighty Saturn when *Cassini* was the subject of assisted suicide.

It was a grand mission by NASA, the European Space Agency, the Italian Space Agency, and the Jet Propulsion Laboratory (JPL) at Caltech, in Pasadena.

An interesting thing about Giovanni Cassini, the famed astronomer, born in Genoa in 1625, is that his first field of study was not astronomy but *astrology*—love of one led to the other.

We are rarely reminded that many of the most storied names in science and invention—Isaac Newton, John Dee, Roger Bacon, Alexander Graham Bell, Thomas Edison, and, of course, Jack Parsons, the occultist and cofounder of the Jet Propulsion Laboratory—were alchemists and magicians.

Jack Parsons grew up in Pasadena with a wild and questing mind. He was building small rockets as a child and would become one of the crucial innovators of rocketry. But his interest in and practice of ritual magick led to his ouster from JPL and Aerojet, which were his creations more than anyone else's, and in 1945 he found himself free to perform magickal rituals full-time.

His frequent partner was none other than L. Ron Hubbard, who had his own career in the U.S. Navy cut short and shared Parsons's interest in science fiction and sorcery. For reasons still in dispute today, and with results that are difficult to prove but do make an interesting argument for themselves, Parsons and Hubbard began a long ritual called the Babalon Working.

The ritual was reportedly completed in the Mojave Desert on January 18, 1946, a completion that would be verified by the appearance of the entity Parsons and Hubbard called the Scarlet Woman. When they returned to Pasadena, she was there waiting, in the form of the artist and muse Marjorie Cameron.

"I returned home," Parsons later wrote, "and found a young woman answering the requirements waiting for me."

She enjoyed the bohemian scene at Parsons's Pasadena lodge on Orange Grove Avenue, but was not originally aware that she had apparently been summoned by ritual magick. Only when she reported her sighting of a luminous disc—possibly the first sighting of the modern flying saucer era—did Parsons and Hubbard let her in on the secret: They had opened a hole in the sky, a hole in space and time. And something, or many things, had come through it.

EULOGY FOR A SPACE MISSION

Jack Parsons died in 1952, allegedly from an accidental explosion in his home laboratory. By the end, he had been betrayed and abandoned by both his rocketry peers and his magickal lodge. L. Ron Hubbard found success as a science fiction writer and eventually as a prophet with his own religion, and Marjorie Cameron lived a long life as an artist and underground star of the occult scene in Los Angeles. Instead of building spaceships, by the end of his life Jack Parsons—an expert chemist and inspired alchemist—was making explosives for Hollywood movies. But NASA and JPL and human spaceflight and even the *Cassini* mission to Saturn do not exist on our timeline without the rocketry genius of Marvel Whiteside Parsons, the pioneer we know as Jack Parsons.

Speaking of Marvel, his given name, if you look at his photographs today—especially the famous shot taken in 1941—the dashing, goateed rocketry-and-chemistry pioneer may well remind you of the Marvel Comics character Tony Stark, the brokenhearted businessman, chemist, and rocketry pioneer who becomes Iron Man, as drawn by the legendary Jack Kirby—who had his own direct connection to the great old gods of space and time. And Jack Parsons will surely bring to mind Tony Stark as portrayed by the actor Robert Downey, Jr.

And those scenes of Afghanistan in 2008's *Iron Man* movie? They were filmed in the Alabama Hills, just off the 395 in the Eastern Sierra desert, the setting for hundreds of movies and television shows about cowboys and superheroes and space monsters.

One of the eeriest desert places you can visit today is called Rocket Site Road, which crosses the old Twenty Mule Team Road south of Boron, at the far end of Edwards Air Force Base, just west of Kramer Junction. There is a jagged, burnt mountain here, clearly visible from the public roadway and studded with the metal hulks of old rocket engines tested by NASA and JPL and the military, bolted to the rock so they wouldn't hurl themselves across the sky.

There was a mysterious explosion at the Rocket Site laboratory on September 7, 1990. A mushroom cloud rose over the lab as a line of ambulances raced down Rocket Site Road. People who lived nearby along Highway 58 were not told the toxic cloud was hydrogen chloride from a multi-rocket-and-missile explosion. The poison cloud dispersed over the Western Mojave.

THE WHITE STAG

North of the rocket factories and windmill farms of Mojave and Tehachapi is a wonderland of piñon trees, mountain streams, and boulder piles called Kelso Valley. For nearly a century, hunters and hikers have reported an enormous albino stag in this remote hunting ground.

This ancestral home of the Tübatulabal at the southern tip of the Sierra Nevada is still known for its mule deer herds, and thousands of Pacific Crest Trail hikers pass through Kelso Valley each year. Wildlife includes black bears, weasels, badgers, bobcats, mountain lions, and a number of permanent and visiting birds.

Since at least the 1930s, there have also been reports of the eerie Kelso Valley Ghost Stag, standing seven feet tall and entirely white, from nose to tail.

"I saw this creature briefly during hunting season," an anonymous witness posted online in 2001. "The albino deer, as we called it, just vanished and was never found, no tracks."

Charles Raymond Dillon's 2001 collection of ghost

stories, *They Came Back*, calls the creature "the Immortal Deer of Shepp Springs," and describes "a deathless deer, a magnificent stag that bullets do not harm." While the Tübatulabal people have many myths and much folklore about the mule deer, what little has been collected and translated does not mention a phantom stag.

Animals leave ghosts behind, too.

Deep inside the old Standard Mine in Bodie—above tree line in the Eastern Sierra—a huge old white-haired mule worked the five-hundred-foot level. After the poor beast of burden was killed when mining cars broke loose, workers on this level began sensing their friend the mule had returned. The senses affected were smell, followed by sight: The odor of their lost companion's droppings would be followed by a close-up apparition of the white mule.

The famed old ghost town of Calico is known for a particular supernatural display on Winter Solstice. According to the *Inland Valley Daily Bulletin* of October 30, 2011, "Human and animal ghosts perform a 'ritual

of some kind' that begins with a bear that moves slowly across the grounds behind Calico Ghost Town."

The best known "ghost of the desert" is the pronghorn, noted for its camouflage and speed. Antelope Valley, now home to Skunk Works and suburbia, earned its name from the immense herds of pronghorn antelope that once roamed there.

APOSTLE OF THE CACTI

Minerva Hamilton Hoyt was a wealthy socialite living in Pasadena, but the death of her infant child and then her husband sent her into the desert wilderness seeking solace and inspiration. She found both, and became a tireless explorer of and advocate for the southwestern deserts. Hoyt became no less than the first great desert conservationist, as crucial to the appreciation and protection of desert landscapes as John Muir was to the High Sierra.

Her life after 1918 was one of dirt-road adventure and big-city campaigns. Hoyt traveled the arid lands and remote canyons in the company of her African American housekeeper. They camped under open skies, exploring the now-famous places that Hoyt would use her money and social status to promote as natural parks.

While best remembered today for her success in convincing Secretary of the Interior Harold Ickes and President Franklin D. Roosevelt to create Joshua Tree National Monument, Hoyt also campaigned for two other vast desert parks that would become reality in her lifetime: Death Valley and Anza-Borrego.

Her influence spread to Mexico's deserts, too: In 1931, the Mexican president Pascual Ortiz Rubio invited Hoyt to suggest desert parks to his administration. Her visits were a media sensation, and Rubio called Hoyt the "apostle of the cacti."

FIGHTING HITLER AND DEFENDING THE DESERT

The California Desert Protection Act became law in October 1994, following a decade of activism and negotiation that graduated Death Valley and Joshua Tree National Monuments to much larger national parks while creating a new national park—Mojave National Preserve—from the old East Mojave National Scenic Area, long administered by the Bureau of Land Management. It created 7.6 million acres of federally protected wilderness, too—close enough to Los Angeles and Las Vegas to be enjoyed by humanity and adding up to what is now the world's second-largest desert preserve.

Senator Alan Cranston, who died back in the year 2000, deeply loved the California desert and introduced the California Desert Protection Act in 1986. It would not become law until 1994, shortly after his retirement resulting from his unfortunate involvement in the savings and loan scandal, and the fate of the bill was unclear until the final hours, when a silver-haired congressman named Jerry Lewis held up the House version until hunting, mining, and off-roading were allowed in the new Mojave park—the reason for the strange use of "preserve" instead of "national park" in its name. Lewis then tried to starve it with a one-dollar annual budget, and rangers had to be loaned out from Death Valley National Park.

Despite these last-minute attacks, the California Desert Protection Act has become a beloved and successful example of wide-scale desert protection that is environmentally sound and economically helpful to the small towns that dot the Mojave.

Back in 1934 when Alan Cranston was a wire-service reporter in Europe, he had a chilling encounter with Adolf Hitler—the same Hitler who would soon be earning a fortune from the sanitized American translation of *Mein Kampf*. Young Alan Cranston translated his own edition. This ten-cent tabloid version—with all

the insane parts intact—sold a half-million copies in ten days.

All proceeds went to refugees from Nazi Germany. But sales were halted and additional copies were shredded after Hitler's New York publisher, Houghton Mifflin, acting on the Führer's behalf, sued Cranston.

In July 1939, the U.S. Circuit Court of Appeals in New York sided with Hitler.

THE HERMIT BALLERINA

When did you first see Death Valley? For me, it was the cold winter of 1982, one of those notorious El Niño winters, and I squeezed into a beat-up Volkswagen Beetle with three high school friends. Somehow we'd all caught Desert Fever. Not Valley Fever, the killer lung fungus common to Phoenix, but Desert Fever: a crazed longing to be far from the stains of human civilization, especially the version of civilization we endure in the California sprawl.

We bounced up the 15 through Barstow and had a 3:00 a.m. breakfast in Baker, at the Bun Boy, plenty of coffee. And then north on Highway 127, as the sky lightened and the white winter sun suddenly topped Kingston Peak, and there it was! I'd never seen anything so vast in my life. Yes, I'd been to the Grand Canyon on a school field trip, when I lived in Arizona, and that is certainly big, but it's big in the wrong direction: down. Here the valley spread out ahead for what must've been hundreds of miles, the road shrinking in the distance, going from wide blacktop ribbon to thin black thread, the Funeral Mountains rising to the northwest, cold gray clouds clotted around the peaks. No sign of another human, no cops, just the four of us, in a Bondo-and-primer falling-apart VW bug with a broken heater fan, thirty degrees Fahrenheit. We parked sideways in the middle of the two-lane highway, got out to breathe that fresh cold desert air, and cracked some beers to greet the day. Miller Genuine Draft, if memory serves.

Whatever the 1980s looked like—pastels and hair gel, mostly—this was the opposite. The thirty-five-millimeter camera I'd borrowed from my dad was loaded with black-and-white film, with Kodachrome color slide film as the backup roll. I stood in the road and took pictures of this ridiculous junker car, my juvenile-delinquent friends using the roof as a beer table.

We were blue-collar romantics, you could say. High school was wrapping up and college was not on the schedule for most of us. We read books and went to punk-rock shows and watched weird movies from the "special interest" section of the local video store. Ronald Reagan was president and that gang was hoping to start the draft again, because of El Salvador and the Sandinistas. Well, at least we had America's national parks to enjoy, for the moment. We wandered through tunnels underneath the old Furnace Creek Inn, but were not welcome in the restaurant because of our general appearance: Those were the days when wearing a pair of Levi's was enough to be refused service at a sit-down restaurant. We sneered at the middle-aged in their pink polo shirts and pressed khaki slacks, and moved on.

But the national park was crowded with snowbirds in their RVs and package tourists pouring out of comfortable buses from Las Vegas, and after hitting the visitor center with its talking dioramas that croaked out *"THE BOYS HAVE COME, THE BOYS HAVE COME!,"* and making the required stops at Scotty's Castle and Badwater, we headed out, back to the place that looked so interesting on the drive in: Death Valley Junction. It looked like a diorama: a whitewashed, dusty Spanish-style plaza holding a run-down hotel with greasy windows, some abandoned rock-and-mineral shops, and, at the end, the Amargosa Opera House.

The place had an eerie feel, that particular feeling that goes with being watched. There were people in there, probably, from the looks of a semifunctional pickup parked nearby and the occasional glance of a face turning away on the other side of those dirty windows. But nobody bothered us, so we walked around and took a lot of pictures and tried various doorknobs, all of which were locked. It was the winter season and the place was not welcoming any visitors. The gas station and garage, across the two-lane highway, had not been operational in a long time. I was still walking around, through the colonnades, when my friends said they were ready to go. I was not sure I wanted to leave at all.

Fifteen years prior, a dancer named Marta Becket found herself in the same place, to get a tire fixed at the filling station, still in operation at the time. She and her husband had been visiting the national monument, and while waiting for repairs at Death Valley Junction, she also fell under the spell of this strange, bright place.

Marta Becket decided to stay. It was 1967, after all. Free spirits from the cold and dreary Northeast were popping up all over the rural West, back to the land, away from the turmoil of the poison cities. She peeked into the old community hall and saw, in her mind's eye, a beautiful theater. She would dance here, she decided, performing her own show.

Marta Becket tracked down the owner of the abandoned Pacific Borax Company town of Death Valley Junction and agreed right then and there to pay forty-five dollars a month in rent for the whole place, which needed a lot of work.

One issue she needed to address was the lack of neighbors, the lack of an audience. And so she painted the audience, over many years, on the walls of the meeting hall she renamed the Amargosa Opera House. These paintings, seen up close, are mildly terrifying. Marta Becket's act was unique and a little terrifying itself, with a creepy clown ballet and the leering faces painted on every flat surface.

That's why I liked it—the idea of it, anyway. All those years of hanging around Death Valley Junction and I never once even tried to see her one-woman show. The idea of it all was quite enough.

Marta Becket was as weird as they come, and she found a place as creepy as her own imagination. There was this shaggy-haired alleged comedian named Tom who arrived after Marta's husband headed out for good,

 and Tom was nearly as weird, serving as Marta's shabby master of ceremonies. Despite doing a good business in tourist season and getting all kinds of mainstream media coverage from the likes of *National Geographic* and the network newsmagazine shows, the place was never maintained, never really repaired. The whole scene was a bit wrong, as would become apparent in later years when Marta Becket's story went from a charming PBS tale of an eccentric artist to something that was probably lingering around the place all along: dark secrets, and, in her old age, whispered claims of senior abuse that occasionally made the local newspapers, and sketchy characters wrangling over her value, in monetary terms.

It's a haunted place in a very real sense: Bad things have happened there, odd things. There are tales of babies buried in the walls, of drownings, of despair and manipulation and loneliness. That is the shadow world of Death Valley Junction, and each night it returns. And if you are there in the night, you will sense it.

But it is also a place of inspiration, a place of hard beauty, a place where certain kinds of people could look around at the auto junkyard and the broken gas pumps and the peeling white plaster piled up around the buildings and say, "This is the place."

Another artist of the time, a bum with a philosophy degree and a Mozart flute, was driving a school bus through Death Valley Junction twice a day when Marta Becket decided to stay. Up at Ash Meadows, which was still a whorehouse at the time and had a nice little barroom, this philosopher waited out the school day under the swamp cooler, putting together his account of being a seasonal park ranger over in Utah in the 1950s. This philosopher and school bus driver, who had published three novels to no particular acclaim, was Edward Abbey, and the book he was working on would be published in 1968 as *Desert Solitaire*.

As for me and my hoodlum friends, we returned to Death Valley and the surrounding wilderness again and again, and on our second trip we found a light on at Death Valley Junction, and we convinced that shaggy character to rent us a room or two for the night, as we had no camping equipment and it was very cold. We bribed him with twenty dollars and a couple of beers, and he pointed us down a dusty, decrepit hallway to a couple of connecting rooms seemingly unchanged since construction was completed in the 1920s. The beds were small and dirty and uncomfortable. There were grotesque paintings leaning here and there, some by Marta and some left from the days of the borax mine. The rooms were unheated and the wind howled through the broken windows. We downed enough beers to sleep but were awoken, repeatedly, by doors creaking open and dresser drawers inching outward and the sounds of footsteps and whispers in the hallway.

In the decades since, a popular form of televised entertainment involves "ghost hunters" bumping around spooky old houses at night, pointing voltage meters at invisible entities and claiming dust balls on their cell-phone photos are "spirit orbs." According to the Internet, many of these people have since brought their ghost meters and reality-TV cameras to Death Valley Junction, and they claim the place is creepy as hell. And they're right.

I've never really gotten the place out of my mind. It met an ideal I had not yet developed: A kind of mental painting of a small compound, all by itself at a High Desert crossroads. A place out of a dream.

Marta Becket performed her farewell in 2012, and kept on ticking until January 30, 2017, when she died at the age of ninety-two. The Amargosa Opera House is her monument and memorial.

OUTLAW IN THE ROCKS

Television's *Star Trek* turned fifty years old in 2016, a Lucille Ball–produced science fiction series that introduced the weird geology of the California desert to generations of Earthlings, as the old western movies and serials had done for earlier generations.

One of the enduring scenes from the original show features William Shatner's Captain James T. Kirk in a melodramatic rock fight with a fierce Lizard Man—a battle that took place at the Vásquez Rocks, those slanted monuments to the San Andreas Fault alongside Highway 14 south of Palmdale. That 1966 episode was called "Arena," and is one of a dozen appearances the Vásquez Rocks made in *Star Trek* productions over half a century.

More than two hundred movies and TV episodes have been shot at the rocks—now a Los Angeles County natural park of 932 acres, with many scenic miles of hiking trails—including dozens of classic westerns and even the 1931 Bela Lugosi version of *Dracula*, in which Southern California geology stood in for Transylvania.

But who was this Vásquez character, anyway?

Tiburcio Vásquez was one of California's "most notorious bandits," a legend of old California.

Born in 1835 at Monterey, then the capital of both Alta and Baja California, Vásquez came from an elite family that arrived with De Anza. He was educated, cultured, charming, and multilingual, and he became a beloved folk hero of oppressed Mexican Californians dismayed by U.S. rule of the Golden State following the Mexican-American War of 1846–48.

An outlaw in Monterey since 1852, by 1870 he was a living legend, moving from rugged hideouts to the society ranchos where he was known for his good looks, elegant manners, excellent dancing, romantic poetry, and skillful guitar playing. The ladies loved him, and he had ongoing affairs with many Californio socialites up and down the state.

One of his last hideouts was the Western Mojave, and he eluded the sheriffs, posses, and vigilantes for months within the wild rocky terrain of the rocks that now bear his name. Here, he began to believe he would never be caught, and made a series of fatal mistakes.

Vásquez was betrayed by one of his lovers while staying at the Los Angeles adobe of "Greek

George" Caralambo, the famed U.S. Army camel driver, whose home stood near today's Sunset Strip in West Hollywood.

Found guilty of murder in San Jose, Tiburcio Vásquez was hanged on March 19, 1875.

The notorious California outlaw was a primary inspiration for the pulp writer Johnston McCulley's Zorro.

MAGIC AND WAR IN LOS ALAMOS WITH WILLIAM S. BURROUGHS

The town of Los Alamos lies upon the slopes of a living supervolcano called the Valles Caldera, at a crisp High-Desert elevation of 7,300 feet above sea level. The modern town is barely a century old, but the nearby cliff villages were built more than a thousand years earlier by the Tewa, who carved homes into the caldera's cliffs—Bandelier Tuff, the chalky volcanic stuff is called, in honor of the archaeologist Adolph Bandelier's work here in the late 1800s.

You can walk among these skull-eyed cliff dwellings—preserved since 1916 within Bandelier National Monument—and appreciate the then-novel approach of Bandelier, who combined "historical research, folklore, mythology, native traditions, ethnography, ethnohistory, and archaeology" in an early effort to remove European-American assumptions about New World culture, as so much more can be discovered with an open mind.

The Swiss-born archaeologist had made early missteps at other New Mexico pueblos, including his witnessing of secret rituals without the community's permission, but in time he learned the humility and careful manners required to learn some of what these Tewa-and-Keres-speaking descendants of the Ancestral Pueblo people already knew. ("Anasazi" is the now out-of-favor Navajo name for this ancient culture that migrated southward from the Four Corners region some seven centuries ago. Drought, dwindling resources, war, and major changes in religion and culture are now thought to be the main reasons for the "vanishing" of the Ancestral Puebloans from the Four Corners.)

Bandelier was led by a Puebloan guide to the ancient dwellings hidden within and around Frijoles Canyon, in the Jemez Mountains, and spent years excavating and studying the pueblo in the valley and numerous brick-fronted cave dwellings in the cliffs above. Mysterious rock art hints at the lives and beliefs of much earlier nomadic peoples on the Pajarito Plateau. From the earliest nomads to the time of the Spanish friars, ritual magic was the crux of daily life. The cliff dwellings reveal a people under constant fear of attack.

Both the Tewa and the Keres chose "War Captains," whose authority combined the power of magicians, commanders, and governors, according to the pioneering anthropologist Elsie Clews Parsons.

"War Captains have ritual functions of prayer and offering, of guarding against witches or intruders, of maintaining the customs, of appointing to office and installing, and of serving as executive messengers," Parsons writes in her two-volume *Pueblo Indian Religion*, published in 1939. "Among Keres and Tewa the War Captains or Outside Chiefs, like Zuni War chiefs, are representatives or proxies for the War Gods and go by their names."

New Mexico became a U.S. state in 1912, a sixty-four-year wait as a "territory" caused in large part by Washington's discomfort with the land's volatile mix of Indian wars, old Mexican society, and a spiritualism entirely foreign to U.S. Protestants, but magic and war would continue to be the primary institutional obsession following statehood.

As Nazism infected the Old World and most of Europe's great physicists collected in the United States, many of them began to suffer nightmare visions of a new weapon that would make Germany unstoppable. Washington must, these celebrated scientists insisted, build the atomic bomb first.

Much of the authority for the Manhattan Project fell to J. Robert Oppenheimer, a wealthy New York–born scientist and suspected communist who had ventured to New Mexico, like so many other elites, for the fashionable "dry air cure" at a guest ranch, in 1922. Oppenheimer's affliction was not tuberculosis, the then-incurable illness that once brought thousands of "lungers" to New Mexico, but dysentery, likely caused by infectious colitis. After the disease kept him bedridden for what was to have been his first year at Harvard, Oppenheimer was taken to New Mexico by his high school English teacher.

Julius Oppenheimer, Robert's father, was a wealthy industrialist and collector of modern art. It was the elder Oppenheimer who suggested the New Mexico trip, believing that "a Western adventure would help to harden his son," according to Kai Bird and Martin J. Sherwin's 2006 biography, *American Prometheus*.

As part of this frontier adventure, the eighteen-year-old Oppenheimer rode from the guest ranch near Cowles to the stark slope of the Pajarito Plateau and across the great caldera. Beyond the old cave dwellings and pueblo, the only permanent settlement was the rough-hewn all-male Los Alamos Ranch School, with its prep-school cowboys doing ranch chores between studies.

Oppenheimer was so taken with the brilliant landscape, the cowboy life, and the arid climate that he later leased (and eventually bought) the little ranch near Cowles for himself. When the need arose for a remote location for America's World War II effort to build the A-bomb, Oppenheimer suggested the part of the desert he loved best: the mountains north of Santa Fe. "My two great loves are physics and New Mexico," he wrote in a letter, and now the two would be combined.

Oppenheimer was also a mystic, not uncommon among the East Coast Americans drawn to New Mexico in the early twentieth century. While his agile mind maneuvered easily through physics both hard and theoretical, there remained a gauze at the frontiers that baffled him. He studied Sanskrit and took to the ancient Hindu texts, a deep interest that poetically merged with his singular profession years later, following the successful Trinity test, the detonation of the first atomic bomb, on July 16, 1945.

It was two decades later when Oppenheimer, abandoned by his government and near death, recalled his thoughts about the A-bomb for NBC television cameras. "We knew the world would not be the same," he said. "A few people laughed, a few people cried, most people were silent. I remembered the line from the Hindu scripture, the Bhagavad-Gita: Vishnu is trying to persuade the Prince that he should do his duty and, to impress him, takes on his multi-armed form and says, 'Now I am become Death, the destroyer of worlds.' I suppose we all thought that, one way or another."

In that ancient story, the human prince Arjuna accepts his responsibility to fight a war he feels is unjust. He is convinced that his profession requires his full participation. Oppenheimer was not suggesting that he

had become Death, the Destroyer of Worlds. Instead, his earthly profession required him to be the war god's proxy. It was Oppenheimer's duty—and because it was his duty, he did not regret the A-bomb's destruction of Hiroshima and Nagasaki.

Oppenheimer's choice for the Manhattan Project's laboratory site, quickly accepted by the U.S. government, was that same picturesque private school he had visited on a horseback camping trip years earlier, set along a creek crowded with Fremont's cottonwoods (*los alamos* in Spanish), on the mesa east of the volcano and west of the Sangre de Cristo mountain range. The climate and views would inspire the great minds called to this duty, he believed.

The final graduating class of the Los Alamos Ranch School rushed to complete their studies by February 1943. The school had been created by a Detroit businessman named Ashley Pond, who had served in Theodore Roosevelt's Rough Riders but avoided combat thanks to a case of typhoid.

The Ranch School's mission was to toughen up the sons of the American elite. Pond believed in the gender segregation some pueblos practiced to create elite warriors. The forest ranger and scoutmaster Pond hired to run the school, A. J. Connell, didn't even want the male teachers to have wives. (An exception was Pond's own wife and daughter—the latter now known as the poet and author Peggy Pond Church, who was shipped off to various girls' boarding schools during the academic year.) The Ranch School educated a number of notable business and artistic figures, including the author Gore

Vidal and John Crosby, founding director of the Santa Fe Opera. The strangest and most brilliant of them all was a boy called Billy Burroughs, grandson of the man who invented the adding machine.

William S. Burroughs was born to a wealthy St. Louis family, but lived a life at odds with the morals and social order of that prim elite. He was a subculture celebrity by the late 1970s and spoke like a wizened Old West card shark. Whether as founder of the Beats with Kerouac and Ginsberg, portraying a priestly old heroin addict in Gus Van Sant's *Drugstore Cowboy*, or creating shotgun art with a disheveled Kurt Cobain, Burroughs dressed like an undertaker, in a rumpled suit—less dapper than shady. Burroughs's writing is packed with studied paranoia regarding government, technology, taboos, and especially the virus of language, which Burroughs believed was the result of deliberate infection by alien "management."

Burroughs and his older brother, Mortimer, attended summer camp at the Los Alamos Ranch School in the years 1925 through 1927. In 1930, sixteen-year-old Burroughs was sent to the school as a full-time student, in part because he suffered sinus problems. Most of the boys were "spindly," sent by rich fathers hoping the desert would toughen them up.

Burroughs begged to come home late in his second year, and later wrote that he loathed the Ranch School's dull chores, cruel classmates, and a headmaster who enjoyed making the students strip naked for him.

But in Burroughs's fiction, especially in later novels such as *The Wild Boys* and *The Place of Dead Roads*, a fantastic version of this Old West–themed all-male school of horseback-riding junior cowboys is the Burroughsian ideal of a perfect society, out of doors and out of control's reach. It is the Los Alamos Ranch School before the A-bomb, the cowboy adolescents without the teachers, without the military men who took over the school, and without the scientists seeking moral justification for bringing the world to the verge of man-made destruction.

Burroughs, interested enough in anthropology to briefly study it at Harvard, enjoyed roaming around the pueblo ruins and cave dwellings. Ted Morgan describes one such ramble in *Literary Outlaw: The Life and Times of William S. Burroughs*: "Rogers Scudder, a St. Louis friend who went to the Ranch School with Billy, also remembers him as wry and sardonic, with a macabre side. He and Billy used to go dig in an old Pueblo Indian ruin . . . Billy found an anthill in the ruin and poured gasoline over it and lit it and started dancing a sort of parody of an Indian war dance, with maniacal whooping as ants by the thousands fled the pyre."

Young Billy Burroughs knew about the war captains, too. He knew about the gods infecting the humans for purposes of war duty. Yet even when he volunteered for the military and the OSS, he was denied. Burroughs attended two of the same elite universities as J. Robert Oppenheimer: Harvard and Columbia, the latter's campus in New York being the original headquarters of both the Manhattan Project and the Beats. Burroughs and Oppenheimer studied many of the same esoteric Eastern texts in their comfortable Cambridge lodgings.

But unlike the War Captains of the pueblos, and unlike Oppenheimer and his ranch school full of world-destroying physicists, Burroughs couldn't do the war gods' duty. His job, it transpired, was to turn the Atomic Age into the darkest comedy. In his best-known books, the still-shocking *Naked Lunch* and the cut-up novel *Nova Express*, the figures of authority are all insane and inept men of privilege, like the sadistic Dr. Benway chopping up patients in some government operating room. "After one look at this planet," Burroughs wrote, "any visitor from outer space would say 'I want to see the manager!'"

THE LANDERS EARTHQUAKE

Do you remember the Landers Earthquake, on June 28, 1992? It was the biggest quake to shake California in nearly seven decades, a magnitude 7.3, officially designated "violent" on the Mercalli scale.

The unincorporated community of Landers—on the northern outskirts of the High Desert town of Yucca Valley, up Highway 247—is a sparsely populated land of Joshua trees and dry rolling hills. It's beautiful up there, and it still feels wild. You might have a nice designer couple from Echo Park in *one* neighboring cabin, but the other two still might house the old High Desert, the one where you could live so cheaply as to entertain the most philosophical approaches to life. Or the most criminal. Landers is something else.

Well, in 1992, there were some artists and nudists and UFO cultists and Buddhists living up around Landers, as is ever the case up there, but mostly there were people who were attracted to the desert life for reasons deep within them, people who perhaps didn't care to talk about such things, people who perhaps had run from something within or without, some hassle, some intractable problem, or maybe just boredom with a pretty dull system, day to day. It was easier in some ways, in 1992: You could still rent a shack or open a savings account without a credit report, you could live on cash dollars, and if all else failed you could cash your social security or military retirement or union pension right at the Stater Brothers, and you could still stop by the SoCal Edison office on the 247 and pay your electric bill with a twenty.

Now you can toss up a couple of solar panels and say goodbye to the utility bill and the fire outages forever, if you want. And you can have a cell phone, if you want. You can sit in your nice old homestead cabin and look at the same television programs as everybody else in every other form of human habitation. It is not so lonely, in that sense. It's four walls (hopefully) on some dirt to call your own, underneath the Milky Way, which you can see even on a quarter-moon night. There are coyotes and nightjars making only the nicest kind of noise out there, if you open the windows.

And when a 7.3 earthquake strikes, even an officially violent one, a benefit of mostly sort-of built-to-code one-story structures far from one another is that a big quake just can't do as much damage to people and their things. Fewer people, fewer things. But there was one fatality of the Landers quake, and it was a sad one: a sleeping child, Joseph R. Bishop, just three-and-a-half years old, was killed by a collapsing fireplace. He was visiting Yucca Valley with his parents.

There were, additionally, more than four hundred injuries. Shop windows exploded, propane fires broke out, one-story buildings were shaken off their slabs or even flattened, and throughout Landers the earth just opened up, gashes across these sandy hills up to eighteen feet across, with vertical displacement of six feet in some spots.

Canyons opened up, in a minute or two of intense shaking, and some homesteaders found their corrals or sheds six feet above the rest of the compound. Highway 247, Old Woman Springs Road—a twisting two-lane highway that's the only way in or out of Landers—even the 247 was torn apart. The north end was jolted up and over a good eight feet, the blacktop crumbled over the break. The water sloshed out of Devils Hole in Death Valley and swimming pools not just out in Los Angeles and Orange County but all the way to Idaho. The geysers at Yellowstone went on a new schedule. And in Landers, there was liquefaction over seismic faults nobody knew existed the day before.

In fact, geologists were in a wild panic because they believed the Landers quake and its powerful aftershocks were just the beginning of the Big One, the overdue San Andreas monster quake that will, one of these days, rip

THE LANDERS EARTHQUAKE

this state apart. The scientists were so convinced the Big One had begun that President Bush, the first one, was rushed back from Camp David to be ready at the White House when Hell opened up in Los Angeles, still in shock from a week straight of riots that burned and scarred L.A. from downtown to Santa Monica. The Big One still hasn't happened.

And seismologists still don't know exactly what the Landers quake meant. One theory is that the San Andreas Fault itself is being *replaced* by a series of faults running up the Mojave Desert and through the Owens Valley and Eastern Sierra, home of Mammoth Mountain, which is a volcano, still warming the hot springs at Benton and Travertine.

The double Ridgecrest temblors in July 2019 did much for the theory that a new major fault is developing between Ridgecrest and Landers.

The whole reason these deserts exist is because of the seismic action that created the Sierra Nevada and the San Bernardino and Tehachapi ranges, the massive walls that turned our interior to desert by holding back the clouds, starving this land of water. Deserts are always lands of little rain, but the way this desert got that way is by the same forces that tore Landers apart almost

thirty years ago: the plates of the Earth, slipping, striking, sliding, and smashing against one another.

And the Mercalli scale? It measures the *intensity* of the quake, the effects of the quake here on the surface. Giuseppe Mercalli, an Italian volcanologist, Catholic priest, and natural sciences professor at Naples, created the Mercalli intensity scale. Imagine the mind of such a person. A geologist priest, living a century ago in Italy, at the dawn of modern geology, studying volcanoes by standing on the edges in the hours (you hoped) before or after an eruption, the sulfur smoke burning your nostrils, a Catholic priest face-to-face with the chaotic, molten energy bursting from the ripped seams of the Earth itself.

The Landers quake was a number IX on this scale, IX of XII, "Violent," and described as: "Damage considerable in specially designed structures; well-designed frame structures thrown out of plumb. Damage great in substantial buildings, with partial collapse. Buildings shifted off foundations. Liquefaction." What follows are three levels of "Extreme," in which railways bend and monuments crumble, stone walls collapse and bridges tumble into rivers, the Earth itself slumps, and there is total destruction. The landscape moves in *waves*, with sightlines distorted and gravity defeated. Massive objects—boulders, trucks, trains—are tossed into the air before crashing down again.

Giuseppe Mercalli died in 1914 in Naples, at the age of sixty-three. He was burned up—burned alive in his bed. Police later revealed that he was murdered over the equivalent of fourteen hundred dollars, about a month's rent if you're lucky, then or now. Soaked in gasoline and burned to death.

An interesting thing happened a few days before the 6.9 Ridgecrest quake of July 4, 2019, and it's enough to make you wonder:

An ancient petroglyph, the Sunburst Petroglyph, was stolen out of a canyon outside of Ridgecrest, from one of those dense concentrations of ancient petroglyphs around Ridgecrest and on the China Lake Naval Weapons Station.

The Sunburst Petroglyph has a diamond pattern of what looks like three brilliant lights or stars, like you're looking up at the underside of one of those black triangles always zooming over the desert, after hovering in place about a hundred feet over the ground, with the spotlight looking around for . . . something.

The person or organization behind this theft of a five-to-six-hundred-pound ancient boulder with this ancient rock art must've gone in with a team of mercenaries or commandos, and maybe a helicopter. Who does something like that? Where did it end up? Maybe in some real-life supervillain's lair, maybe in one of those vulgar high-rise apartment buildings above the Las Vegas Strip.

What is known is that the two big Ridgecrest quakes of 2019, on July 4 and then the 7.1 quake of July 5, came less than a week after the Bureau of Land Management's announcement of the petroglyph theft, on June 28.

The whole desert around Ridgecrest and China Lake has been shaking and rocking ever since. We better find that Sunburst Petroglyph and put it back, right back where it belongs.

HIDDEN CITIES AND SECRET CREATURES OF DEATH VALLEY

Deep into the weird year of 1947, a man named Howard E. Hill stood before a lunchtime audience at the Los Angeles Transportation Club and told an incredible tale of an ancient temple within Death Valley's Panamint Mountains.

Hill spoke on behalf of Dr. F. Bruce Russell, who had retired his medical practice in Ohio to mine the California desert for treasure. The desert Southwest was filling up with aging easterners seeking dry air for their various ailments and excitement for their dull lives.

Dr. Russell had found both, but for years he had little luck in convincing the world to accept his Death Valley discovery. That became Howard Hill's job, the fruits of which could be found in newspapers across America in the days following the announcement.

On August 4, 1947, the Associated Press sent out a story that began with this:

LOS ANGELES—A retired Ohio doctor has discovered relics of an ancient civilization, whose men were 8 or 9 feet tall, in the Colorado desert near the Arizona-Nevada-California line. Several well-preserved mummies were taken from caverns in an area roughly 180 miles square, extending through much of southern Nevada from Death Valley, California, and across the Colorado River into Arizona.

Dr. Russell claimed that in 1931, he had fallen through loose alluvial sands into an underground cavern while he was digging a mine shaft. He returned in 1946 with an Arizona-born archaeologist named Daniel S. Bovee, who had worked on cliff-dwelling sites in New Mexico and claimed to be an expert in Native American history.

Bovee and Russell entered the remote Panamint cavern and explored for many days, counting thirty-two lengthy tunnels and allegedly discovering many mummified remains of a race of giants. Preserved in the cool, dry caves, the mummies were clad in suits of tailored animal skins, along with the "implements of the civilization." Remains of mammoths and saber-toothed cats were said to line another subterranean tunnel.

The media sensation was short-lived. Anthropologists found the tale ridiculous, especially Hill's claims that one great chamber featured "devices and markings similar to those now used by the Masonic order." Hill and Russell vanished from the public eye. Daniel S. Bovee died in Laguna Beach in 1983, his career in fringe archaeology forgotten.

It was not the first claim of mummies and lost civilizations discovered beneath the Panamint Mountains. Bourke Lee, collector of Death Valley folklore, had, in 1932, related a tale he heard from the miners Bill Cocoran and Jack Stewart, who had made the acquaintance of three individuals having car trouble on the highway beyond Furnace Creek: Fred Thomason and a "Mr. & Mrs. White."

Thomason and Mr. White had also fallen through alluvial sands, near Wingate Pass, and found themselves in a chamber of wonders.

Giants are not mentioned in this tale, which you can read in the pages of Lee's book *Death Valley Men*. These lucky men had discovered an underground city of gold.

The reported location of the shaft is at the southern end of the Panamints. The year of discovery is uncertain; Bourke Lee places the event in "the 1920s."

It is best to let Mr. White describe the scene:

Gold spears! Gold shields! Gold statues! Jewelry! Thick gold bands on their arms! I found them! I fell into the underground city. There was an enormous room, big as this canyon. A hundred men were in it. Some were sitting around a polished table that was inlaid with gold and precious stones. Men stood around the walls of the room carrying shields and spears of solid gold. All the men—more than a hundred men—had on leather aprons, the finest kind of leather, soft and full of gold ornaments and jewels. They sat there and stood there with all that wealth around them. They are still there. They are all dead!

The tunnels and chambers within those mountains eventually climbed thousands of feet above the green splotch of Furnace Creek, on Death Valley's floor, which the men claimed to be able to see through great open windows that met what appeared to be the smooth stone of boat landings, great docks that once met the ancient waters of Lake Manly.

Frustrated by their attempts to sell the discovery to the Smithsonian for a fair price—just five million dollars for a treasure surely worth billions—the men claimed to have attracted some interest from the Southwest Museum, in Los Angeles. But violent flash floods had "changed the country all around," and they were unable to find the cavern entrance again.

It is the sort of story you sometimes hear after the whiskey has been passed around the campfire too many times, especially when hard-luck miners are in attendance. But at least one local Indian told a similar tale, also shared in Bourke Lee's book: "A Timbisha guide named Tom Wilson claimed his grandfather entered an unknown tunnel along the Panamints and disappeared for three entire years."

When he returned, he described a strange people who lived within the mountains and spoke an unknown language. They rode horses through the miles-long tunnels and dined well on foods unknown to Death Valley foragers. The grandfather was treated kindly and welcomed to stay, but eventually chose to return to his tribe. Tom Wilson had sought the entrance to this other world ever since.

John Wesley Powell, the great explorer of the Colorado River, was told a similar story in the 1860s while navigating the Grand Canyon. But in this version, the tribal elder was seeking his dead wife in an underworld peopled by a strange race. Powell was reportedly shocked, as the tale was nearly identical to the Greek legend of Orpheus and Eurydice.

Wingate Pass is five miles due south of the Manson Family's last hideout, at Barker Ranch. And Charles Manson's proximity to Wingate Pass in 1968 and '69 is more than a morbid footnote: Manson was obsessed with the underground caverns around Death Valley, convinced he could find a hole like Devils Hole that would allow him and his followers to drop out of sight and wait out the apocalyptic race war he hoped to begin with the Los Angeles murder rampage he orchestrated in August 1969. Afterward, the Family retreated to Barker Ranch, with Manson hoping police would blame the ritual murders on the Black Panthers, setting "Helter Skelter" into motion.

In Saline Valley, now within Death Valley National Park's northern boundaries, Manson was delighted to find a hot-spring pool with no apparent bottom. He ordered Steve Grogan and Ruth Ann Moorehouse to dive down and find the floor, but the water was too hot. They instead attached a stone to a rope and tried to determine the pool's depth. They failed to get an accurate reading.

Manson couldn't stop thinking about the subterranean paradise. He knew about the rumored caverns and mummies; they were mentioned on the TV show *Death Valley Days*. He knew that in 1965, three young men had descended into Devils Hole, on the other side of Death Valley. And he knew that two of those divers did not come out of the hole. It was all over the news for weeks, especially as teams of experienced scuba divers went deep into the fossil waters and came back with nothing beyond a snorkeling mask and a flashlight left as an exit marker. Where did those young men go?

For three days in 1968, Manson reportedly meditated at Devils Hole, waiting for a sign, a clue, a revelation.

One of Manson's death squad, Tex Watson, described it like this: "While the rich piggies lay butchered on their own manicured front lawns, we would have found safety. Charlie would have led us through a secret Devils Hole into the Bottomless Pit: an underground paradise beneath Death Valley, where water from a lake would give everlasting life and you could eat fruit from 12 magical trees—a different one for each month of the year. That would be Charlie's gift to us, his children, his Family."

Claims of ancient giants were not uncommon in the United States, especially in the westward expansion of the 1800s. The sites of the great mound civilizations of the Ohio River Valley and Mississippi Valley were said to hold the graves of an old race of ten-foot-tall warrior kings, although the skeletons tended to mysteriously disappear or be revealed as hoaxes. Joseph Smith, the founder of the Latter-Day Saints, was one of those who claimed to know a secret history of prehistoric America.

Like the many tales of blue-eyed ancient Americans with blond or red hair, there was a strong racist element to such stories, an insistence that North America's indigenous tribes must have arrived after a superior white race had died out, or gone back to Egypt of the pharaohs or Crete of the Minoans.

On California's Channel Islands, a grave robber named Ralph Glidden exhumed thousands of Native American skeletons and built an entire museum on Catalina Island from those bones. Skulls were used as lamps in the crude building, holding electric light fixtures. Windows were edged in bones from toes, ankles, wrists, and fingers, and human vertebrae lined the ceiling. Glidden swore he had also discovered giants, the skeletons of which were somehow "evidence of a prehistoric race of giant fair-skinned, blue-eyed natives." Catalina Island's owners, the Wrigley family, later bought the morbid museum and its desecrated remains. Most of those ransacked remains eventually found their way to the hidden archives of UCLA's Fowler Museum.

In Death Valley, at least, it was allowed that the ancient subterranean civilization was related to the Timbisha Shoshone tribe that inhabits the region today, although Shoshone people likely arrived after the Fremont culture was displaced, around a thousand years ago.

Shoshone folklore tells of their coming into contact with a red-haired tribe of fierce cannibals they called the "tule dwellers." And the discoveries at Nevada's Lovelock Cave and the Black Rock Desert provided much evidence for a rich Lake Lahontan culture, shown in artifacts such as the ten-thousand-year-old sandals known as the New World's oldest surviving shoes, and the collection of beautifully detailed duck decoys made from tule and decorated with feathers. As the great inland seas of the Pleistocene began to recede—including Lake Manly and Lake Panamint, within the boundaries of today's Death Valley National Park—the tule dwellers moved on or died out. Perhaps they were the mysterious cave people. The human remains at Lovelock Cave had been too scattered and disturbed to legitimize claims that giants had been buried there, and the bits of red hair claimed to have been collected at such sites have been explained away as the result of oxidization and discoloration of the original black hair. Still, there are the sandals: A pair displayed in a Reno museum in the 1950s matched a men's U.S. size 15.

Sarah Winnemucca, the famed nineteenth-century Paiute author and activist, wrote down many Paiute and Shoshone legends and oral histories for the first time. In the small world of giant enthusiasts at the fringes of archaeology and anthropology, she is often quoted as a source for the reality of the red-haired giant cannibals who

warred with her people in the centuries before her time. And such quotes are almost accurate, as Winnemucca does describe a long war with a cannibal race, and how the Paiute forced this enemy tribe to retreat on tule rafts onto Humboldt Lake, and how her ancestors eventually chased the enemy into Lovelock Cave and set a fire at the entrance.

"My people say that the tribe we exterminated had reddish hair," she writes in 1883's *Life Among the Paiutes: Their Wrongs and Claims*. "I have some of their hair, which has been handed down from father to son. I have a dress which has been in our family a great many years, trimmed with this reddish hair. I am going to wear it some time when I lecture. It is called the mourning dress, and no one has such a dress but my family."

She did not, however, describe this vanquished cannibal race as being any taller than regular people. Andrew White, an anthropologist with a particular passion for deflating claims of ancient North American giants, notes that the only time Sarah Winnemucca wrote of giants was in the clear context of legend. In chapter 2, "Domestic and Social Moralities," she writes that Paiute parents tell their children "love stories, stories of giants, and fables—and when they ask if these last stories are true, they answer, 'Oh, it is only Coyote,' which means that they are make-believe stories."

But in 1931, according to a clipping from the *Lovelock Review-Miner*, the remains of two enormous beings were reportedly discovered in the Humboldt dry lake bed. The shorter of the two, at eight foot six, was said to be dressed in strips of gummed cloth, like an Egyptian mummy. The second giant, ten feet in height, was found four months later, in June 1931.

Dr. F. Bruce Russell claimed he fell into a tomb of giants in Death Valley later that same year.

One of the many curious facts about the Mojave Desert is that great underground rivers and lakes still abound beneath this sun-blasted, dried-up surface. The Mojave River itself, with headwaters in the San Bernardino Mountains, makes only a few year-round appearances at the surface—the Narrows at Lane Crossing and again at Afton Canyon—before draining into the mineral sands beyond Zzyzx.

When deep earthquakes rock Mexico and Alaska, the waters are violently disturbed at Devils Hole in Death Valley: the 7.9 Gulf of Alaska quake on January 23, 2018, created foot-tall waves in the pupfish pool, while an 8.1 temblor in Chiapas on September 8, 2017, caused three-foot-tall waves that knocked plants off the usually dry sides of Devils Hole. Fresh waters flow beneath the usually dry 185 miles of the Amargosa River, too, and wildlife conservationists have proven that the Mojave Desert freshwater aquifer targeted by the Cadiz Corporation feeds dozens of surface springs that keep wildlife alive, especially our protected desert bighorn sheep.

These geologic and hydrological facts, in large part unknown a century ago, give some credence to the stories of miners stumbling upon underground rivers alongside the remnants of ancient cultures. (The great archaeological dig at Lovelock Cave, in the Great Basin, was an accidental discovery by guano miners in 1911, as was the unearthing of the Nag Hammadi gnostic gospels in 1945 Egypt.)

These underground rivers and lakes lend some plausibility to a persistent legend from the Death Valley Timbisha: that another race of beings lives within the Panamint Mountains to this day, and that these beings travel in great canoes across the sky.

Howard E. Hill's wild presentation at the Los Angeles Transportation Club barely registers on the list of oddities in the news of 1947. That was the year flying saucers entered (and never left) the American consciousness. Kenneth Arnold—a private pilot and western U.S. businessman—watched a formation of nine shiny, boomerang-shaped aircraft zip over Mount Rainier on June 24, 1947. The crafts' bizarre movement from point to point across the sky reminded him of the way a flat stone or tea saucer would skip on the surface of a pond. It was an editor's choice to translate this description of movement into a description of the objects themselves. And distinctively shaped "flying saucers" were soon being reported around the world—especially in the Mojave Desert outside of Los Angeles. George Van Tassel's UFO conventions at Giant Rock drew thousands of believers and hucksters from Los Angeles and beyond. Van Tassel's fellow alien contactees were often called to the Mojave to greet the spaceships.

Kenneth Arnold wrote his first-person account of

his flight among the flying saucers in the premiere issue of *Fate*, the new pulp magazine created by the visionary Ray Palmer, previously editor at *Amazing Stories*. UFO lore from a Timbisha elder was exactly the kind of material that would make *Fate* an instant success with readers whose view of the world had been severely shaken by the Nazis, the atomic bomb, and the haunting lights and impossibly fast aircraft flying unmolested over the United States in the late 1940s.

"Tribal Memories of the Flying Saucers" appeared in the September 1949 issue and was credited to a Navajo writer named "Oga-Make," a pen name of one of Ray Palmer's frequent contributors: Lucile Taylor Hansen. She used the byline L. Taylor Hansen in her articles about American Indian religious traditions, and in *Fate* this interest would merge with the flying saucer craze, with a Timbisha elder explaining the long history of anomalous lights over Death Valley—the Shoshone name for the land being Tomesha.

"We have known of these ships for untold generations," says the unnamed elder. "We also believe that we know something of the people who fly them. They are called the Hav-musuvs. They are a people of the Panamints, and they are as ancient as Tomesha itself."

It is a story of catastrophic climate change.

"Living within their mountain fortress, the Hav-musuvs ruled the inland sea, trading with far-away peoples and bringing strange goods to the great docks said to still exist in the caverns. As the centuries rolled past, the climate began to change. The water in the lake went down until there was no longer a way to the sea, and only a dry crust remained of the great blue lake. The Fire-God began to walk across Tomesha, the Flaming Land."

As in the extraterrestrial lore of the twentieth century and the fairy lore of old Europe, the Hav-musuvs are beautiful people dressed in white, with long and lustrous hair. "Their skin is a golden tint," says the elder, and it brings to mind George Van Tassel's space visitors with their "good healthy tans." But like their alien-gray and elven cousins, they should not be annoyed or pursued. The elder says: "These strange people have weapons. One is a small tube which stuns one with a prickly feeling like a rain of cactus needles. One cannot move for hours, and during this time the mysterious ones vanish up the cliffs. The other weapon is deadly. It is a long, silvery tube. When this is pointed at you, death follows immediately."

MARTY ROBBINS ON THE COWBOY TRAIL FROM PHOENIX TO EL PASO

Marty Robbins grew up poor on the Arizona desert, mostly living in tents and lean-to shacks on the outskirts of Glendale. His father was Polish, his mother mostly Paiute Indian, his siblings numerous. With no money for a tree, the kids once decorated a creosote bush for Christmas.

It was 1937 when eleven-year-old Martin David Robinson used money earned from picking cotton to see a Gene Autry singing-cowboy movie, *Yodelin' Kid from Pine Ridge*. The suave, impeccably dressed California cowboy singer immediately became Robbins's hero, and Robbins spent a day at the movie theater in Glendale watching Gene Autry whenever he could afford the dime. After happily sitting through every showing until the place closed, Robbins walked the ten miles home in the dark.

"The desert's full of rattlesnakes, centipedes, scorpions, sidewinders," he told an interviewer decades later. "But it didn't bother me. I was Gene Autry."

Robbins worked as a laborer and cowboy on the ranches around Phoenix, but the authentic experience was all grueling work and very little money. Hopping freight trains, hustling in pool halls, and other petty crimes occupied his time until he dropped out of Glendale High and joined the navy. He somehow managed to learn the guitar and develop his singing voice during this hardscrabble Great Depression childhood in a Salt River Valley that few twenty-first-century Phoenicians would recognize as home.

After returning home from World War II, Robbins began finding work in the honky-tonks, and he sang his way into a job hosting his own western-music radio program and then hosting a local television show. Those who lived in 1950s Phoenix speak with pride about their local cowboy hero, who by 1957 was recording number-one hits in both Nashville and New York while starring in his own Hollywood westerns, including *Raiders of Old California.*

Western music and the singing cowboys had peaked in American culture twenty years earlier, but Robbins remained loyal. After his retro-cowboy theme song to the Gary Cooper movie *The Hanging Tree* became a hit, in early 1959, Robbins had his chance to make a whole album of such material, including four haunting narrative songs he composed: "Big Iron," "In the Valley," "His Master's Call," and "El Paso."

There are variations, but the story usually goes like this: Compelled by his success to relocate to Nashville in the early 1950s, Robbins and his family—wife Marizona, son Ronny, and daughter Janet, born in 1959—

always drove back to Arizona at Christmastime. During these long drives across the open-sky country of New Mexico and West Texas, sometimes Marty would lounge in the back seat of his turquoise Cadillac with a guitar, playing with song ideas while Marizona drove.

"Daddy was in the back seat with his little guitar and a yellow legal pad just writing down words as fast and furiously as he could," Ronny Robbins recalled for the *Phoenix New Times* in the spring of 2000. "And I'm thinking, 'Man, that song is like a movie.'"

Marty Robbins himself remembers tinkering with "El Paso" over the course of several holiday drives back and forth to Phoenix, with the welcome sign outside "the City of El Paso" triggering the song's title and refrain. Having worked with the best session musicians and producers in New York and Nashville, Robbins knew the sound he wanted for his western-songs collection: sparse, evocative, as romantic and adventurous as the *ranchera* ballads the Mexican men sang at night by the railroad tracks back in the Glendale barrio.

Columbia Records executives unenthusiastically budgeted a single day of recording time for the twelve-song record that would become known to the world as *Gunfighter Ballads and Trail Songs*.

Accompanying his own magnificent voice and guitar strumming, Robbins had the already legendary Grady Martin picking clean Spanish acoustic, along with Robbins's longtime touring guitarist, Jack Pruett. The haunting background vocals, which float around the action and then soar up with Robbins's voice, are the work of the Glaser Brothers, an act Robbins had signed to his own label two years earlier. The bassist Bob Moore, another player from Grady Martin's 1950s A-team, handles "El Paso" without a drummer; Louis Dunn provides gentle percussion when the other songs require it. The arrangements are so rich, the mastery of the material so complete, that it's difficult to consider this greatest album in the history of cowboy songs as being recorded live by the London-born Columbia staff producer Don Law in a single day.

"El Paso," while two minutes longer than the standard pop and country singles, became a monster crossover hit and was awarded the first Grammy in the category of country music. The album went on to sell more than a million copies, its iconic black-on-red cover seen where country albums had rarely been seen before. Few collections of songs have ever had such a deep and meaningful impact in American recorded music, and few albums have ever sounded so purely evocative.

Robbins brought romantic cowboy balladry back to the charts, and caused a wave of hit story songs in the "El Paso" vein that thrived in the early 1960s—songs such as Johnny Horton's tall tale "The Battle of New Orleans," which also featured Grady Martin's guitar lines. After the success of *Gunfighter Ballads*, country concept albums would follow by ambitious artists such as Johnny Cash, Willie Nelson, and Merle Haggard (who even named his son "Marty" in Robbins's honor). But the record had a deep influence on the rock, outlaw country, and folk-rock acts that found success in the middle and late 1960s, too.

Bob Dylan, who had invented a desert hobo biography for himself that sounded right out of Robbins's trail songs of 1959, paid explicit tribute in 1965's "Desolation Row," a Beat-poet take on a border song with the new Nashville hotshot multi-instrumentalist Charlie McCoy playing Spanish-cowboy lines like Grady Martin's. And the Grateful Dead—who played "El Paso" at nearly four hundred concerts—found their own gunfighter ballad in "Friend of the Devil," which follows an outlaw with a whole Marty Robbins album's worth of trouble on his trail: the devil, the sheriff, a pack of hounds, a child of questionable paternity, and a couple of wives in different cowboy towns.

Like all great music of and about the American desert, Marty Robbins's *Gunfighter Ballads and Trail Songs* is best appreciated outside a desert cabin on a summer night, with coyote howls and gusts of wind upsetting the dog now and then.

EDWARD ABBEY'S ODE TO SOLITUDE

Death Valley High School got a new bus driver in the fall of 1966. He was overqualified, with a master's degree in philosophy from the University of New Mexico, and he was broke again. Edward Abbey had published a couple of novels to little notice, although his postmodern western *The Brave Cowboy* had been adapted into an interesting black-and-white movie with Kirk Douglas called *Lonely Are the Brave*.

Pushing forty and owing child support, the wandering philosopher took whatever public-sector job he could get: seasonal park ranger, fire lookout, social worker, school bus driver. Few remembered him in Shoshone and Furnace Creek. He wasn't there long.

But in a corner of the saloon attached to the legal brothel at Ash Meadows, just across the Nevada line, the underemployed park ranger and philosopher worked on a new manuscript. His novels weren't selling and his agent in New York suggested something different.

Maybe nonfiction, maybe some of Abbey's barroom tales about camping.

Abbey had filled many notebooks during his 1950s summer jobs as the one and only on-site ranger at what was then called Arches National Monument, in the canyon country just north of Moab, Utah. It was an ideal life for a writer who needed the solitude and drama of a wild desert landscape. Sometimes he was there alone, living in a little plywood-and-tin house trailer off a dirt road just north of Balanced Rock. Sometimes his wife and baby lived there with him. The book that was born from those journals, first published a half century ago by McGraw-Hill, made it very clear that Edward Abbey preferred the time alone.

Desert Solitaire, published to little promotion and few sales in January 1968, told the story of an American wanderer from Appalachian Pennsylvania finding his place in the remaining wild parts of the American West. It was good prose, plain and descriptive at times, comic or romantic when necessary. He was writing about the 1950s in the 1960s, and he was still formal enough to win approval from the East Coast elite: In *The New York Times*, Edwin Way Teale described the book as a "wild ride on a bucking bronco" and the author as "a rebel, an eloquent loner."

There were stories of finding a dead tourist under a lone juniper tree, luring a moon-eyed horse from a canyon, guzzling near beer with Mormon uranium miners at a Moab honky-tonk, and walking the lonesome trails of Arches when few visited this remote preserve at the end of a rutted dirt road.

The stories and multiple seasons combine into one staggeringly beautiful High Desert summer in a landscape that demands contemplation. Why set aside natural places as wilderness, preserves, and national monuments? Why should the philosophical and aesthetic value of wild nature occasionally prevail over the corporate interests that only see the landscape as opportunities for strip-mining, for industrial tourism, for fracking? Edward Abbey's answers were individualistic and perversely contradictory. A rattlesnake's life is worth more than a man's, he insists, and then he brains a cottontail with a rock. As an experiment in self-reliance. The park ranger feels horror and shame, watching the quivering bunny die. But then he feels the satisfaction of knowing he could live off the land, if he had to: "The experiment was a complete success. It will never be necessary to perform it again."

The ecology movement began in 1962, with Rachel Carson's *Silent Spring*. The pollution-belching factories, dead rivers, and open garbage dumps were finally seen as public dangers, and the sudden disappearance of wildlife—even the bald eagle was close to extinction!—shocked the nation into action. It was Richard Nixon's administration, of all things, that would launch the Environmental Protection Agency, the Endangered Species Act, the Clean Air Act, and the Clean Water Act. But Abbey said we needed wilderness because *we needed wilderness*. Because true wilderness provided a haven for outlaws.

He claimed to be an anarchist, a man against the state, yet his life's work was dedicated to federal protection of desert wilderness. Three years after the first edition of *Desert Solitaire* came and went, with its few encouraging reviews, the book was out of print and Edward Abbey was again making ends meet with seasonal fire-lookout and ranger work.

That's when the paperback edition appeared, and it was quickly embraced by hordes of long-haired backpackers filling the national parks of the Southwest. Abbey, a loner and rhetorical extremist, struck a nerve with a communal movement of positive people young enough to be his children. A battered copy of *Desert Solitaire* in a backpack was a philosophical weapon against the industrial-capitalist state that had replaced citizens with consumers. It signified that the reader loved wilderness for the sake of wilderness.

Never a bestseller, the book was something nearly as good for a working writer: a steady seller. Robert Redford and the Arizona governor Bruce Babbitt loved the book, befriended the author, and spread its message in policy and culture. *Solitaire* inspired action in its fans, too. They demanded more protected wilderness, and railed against traffic-jammed roads in these sacred spaces, traffic jams we still suffer in Zion and Yosemite and Joshua Tree.

By the mid-1970s, Edward Abbey had fans of the rock-music variety, who showed up at his house, sent love letters, even found the lonely little fire-lookout towers where he now worked not so much out of financial necessity but for silence, privacy, inspiration, solitude. His journals, eventually published as *Confessions of a Barbarian*, reveal how much he desired real literary fame, the acceptance and love of the New York crowd he claimed to disdain, and material riches so he could build a nice house somewhere in remote Utah or Arizona, so he could stop worrying about child support and publishers turning down manuscripts. It never happened. "Cactus Ed" had a shabby and peculiar fame, which meant he was a working writer up until the end. Edward Abbey died in 1989, at the age of sixty-two.

The desert around Joshua Tree has come into fashion, and Ed Abbey's half-century-old book is often seen on the bookshelves of vacation cabins and desert park gift shops. It is one of those books that can catch a reader on any page, with a rant against industrial tourism or a supernaturally tinged tale of wandering a canyon alone or a humorous remembrance of some misadventure. And just like that, you are converted. You are a desert lover, a desert defender, whether as a weekend pursuit or a full-time life. Protecting the wild desert becomes your moral priority. Desert conservation groups from Moab to the Mojave are made of *Desert Solitaire* readers, and most of them can tell you how it changed their lives and work, how it focused and sharpened a mission they had felt stirring but could not yet articulate. *Desert Solitaire* gives a reader the courage to act, and consoles you when your side—the moral side, the moral majority—loses a battle.

A half century after *Solitaire*, you can look at a map of the Southwest and find ample evidence that things are now both worse and better. The people never quit coming west, feeding the monster sprawl of Salt Lake City and Las Vegas, Phoenix and Tucson, the Coachella Valley and the Antelope Valley. There is not nearly enough water for all these people, and thirsty cities are draining distant aquifers and rare desert springs in attempts to continue development, feed the cancer, forever extend the endless traffic-clogged boulevards of strip malls and tract homes and casino-hotels and golf courses. Species are still fading out, from loss of habitat and climate change. We face, of course, imminent extinction ourselves, whether by nuclear winter or endless summer.

Yet there are tens of millions more acres of protected natural desert in California now, post–*Desert Solitaire*, and the connected parks and monuments and designated wilderness from Death Valley down to Joshua Tree now make up the second-largest desert preserve on Earth. (The largest is Namib-Naukluft National Park, in southwest Africa.) But these U.S. preserves and parks are no longer safe from their own protectors. The West's public lands are not treasures to the vile creeps who took power in January 2017 but assets to sell and to steal, to hand over to the petroleum and coal industries. California's beloved new desert national monuments were immediately targeted by the administration's man at the Department of the Interior, the since-departed Ryan Zinke. It was Zinke who, between luxury travel at your expense and well-compensated pep talks to fossil-fuel lobbyists, sought to destroy California's Desert Renewable Energy Conservation Plan, which had saved millions of acres of wild desert from industrial development. It was Zinke who wanted personal authority to build gas pipelines through national parks, an immoral policy embraced by his loathsome successor, David Bernhardt. Land conservationists suffered the realization that giving privately purchased land preserves to the American government for safekeeping is no longer a sure thing. The enemy has no moral obligation to respect the sanctuary of the vanquished.

The Nevada brothel where Abbey scribbled away his days lies in ruins now, alongside a privately owned rock quarry surrounded by Ash Meadows National Wildlife Refuge—land that serves as a pretty good memorial for *Desert Solitaire*. Ash Meadows, a rare desert wetland with twenty species of plants and animals found nowhere else, was purchased by the Nature Conservancy in 1983—more than thirteen thousand acres that were about to be converted into a housing development. It was given to the U.S. government, in the belief that it would be protected forever.

For now, it's the Ash Meadows National Wildlife Refuge. There's an Abbey quote on the wall of the visitor center, by the restrooms.

RAMBLING AROUND WITH ED ABBEY

Edward Abbey died in 1989 and still shows no signs of going quietly. Three decades after his death, Abbey looms over southwestern culture, his paperbacks always prominently displayed in desert cabins and independent bookshops, his grinning and grizzled image on T-shirts and coffee mugs and magazine covers. A recent documentary about the Earth First! movement he inspired plays to sellout crowds at land-conservation fundraisers.

There are as many books about Edward Abbey as there are books *by* Edward Abbey.

For those of us who can recall when he still walked the Earth, it seems less like an Abbey revival than a slow boil of his beloved Slumgullion Stew, the campfire pot bubbling with beans and onions and bacon and whatever else was within reach. The Cactus Ed of 2015 is a weird mix of environmentalist icon and libertarian hero, a pickup-driving lecher who swilled beer and loved symphonies, an overeducated intellectual from an Appalachian family of hillbilly socialists, an Old Testament prophet leering over the old television set he just shot a hole through, an anti-government crank who tirelessly advocated for federal protection of the desert wilderness and spent most of his life hustling one government job after another, an anti-immigration nut in Arizona who once edited a bilingual newspaper and might even be buried in Mexico.

Let it all simmer for thirty years and it becomes the whole American desert, with its starkly gorgeous landscapes and beautiful myths and stucco strip malls and endless political jabbering about the same half dozen subjects. Abbey made his art from all of that: the desert so vast yet so vulnerable, high culture and low culture and no culture, country songs and western movies, flute concertos and European philosophy, Coors cans bouncing off the asphalt and into the Russian thistle, Baskin-Robbins girls in air-conditioned shopping centers, and hairy old satyrs drunk around the campfire again. Death Valley in Eastern California, Big Bend country in West Texas, and especially all the deserts, rivers, slickrock, mountains, and canyons of the Four Corners and northern Mexico—that's what Ed Abbey considered his real home. He wrote so well about these places and their various creatures (javelinas, park rangers, Mormons, vultures, rednecks, the "rosy-bottomed skinny dipper," etc.) that all of arid North America can feel like Abbey's Country. As he intended.

For the reader of Edward Abbey's prose, the place names alone bring whole scenes to mind. *Flagstaff*: Hay-

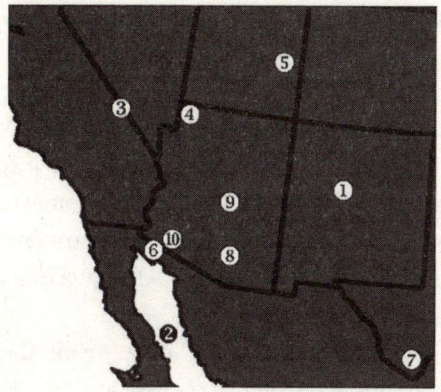

TEN STOPS ON ABBEY'S ROADS

1. **University of New Mexico, Albuquerque**
2. **Isla Ángel de la Guarda, Sea of Cortez**
3. **Death Valley, California, and Ash Meadows, Nevada**
4. **Wolf Hole, Arizona**
5. **Arches National Park and Moab, Utah**
6. **El Pinacate y Gran Desierto de Altar Biosphere Reserve, Sonora**
7. **Big Bend National Park, Texas**
8. **Tucson, Arizona**
9. **Aztec Peak, Arizona**
10. **Cabeza Prieta National Wildlife Refuge, Arizona**

duke avenges the real Abbey's long-ago arrest for vagrancy. *Lee's Ferry*: where that gang of happy saboteurs meets up. *Green River, Aravaipa Canyon, Molly's Nipple*—place names full of romance and adventure. How about ten more?

RAMBLING AROUND WITH ED ABBEY

1. ALBUQUERQUE, NEW MEXICO

It was the Four Corners country that first captivated young Abbey when he rode a freight train in the hobo style, looking out upon the vast New Mexico landscape from an open boxcar. Once free of his military obligations and with a few semesters of college back in Pennsylvania, Abbey transferred to the University of New Mexico in Albuquerque as a beneficiary of the G.I. Bill.

Abbey lived all around town, from the student barracks at Kirtland Air Force Base to shared apartments close to campus to various old adobes and cheap cinder-block cabins in the Sandia foothills and around Tijeras Canyon. It was at UNM that Abbey got into his first trouble as a writer, as editor of the student literary magazine *The Thunderbird*.

As the *Daily Lobo* reported on April 5, 1951, the magazine was suspended by school authorities "as a result of the cover of *The Thunderbird*'s March issue. On it was the phrase 'Man will never be free until the last king is strangled with the entrails of the last priest.' The statement was falsely attributed to Louisa May Alcott. Canceling the May issue of *The Thunderbird*, the order ends the job of the magazine's editor, Edward Abbey."

The Thunderbird is long gone, as are most of the establishments Abbey was known to have frequented. One he mentioned by name was "Okie Joe's." This Route 66 bar and BBQ restaurant once stood at 1720 Central Avenue SE, catty-corner from the University of New Mexico's beloved Lobo statue. Now it's a charmless 7-Eleven minimart and gas station, adding to the general strip-mall ambiance of the UNM neighborhood.

Abbey and his beatnik friends downed many a ten-cent mug of beer at Okie Joe's, then a male-only dive. There's nothing quite like it today, although a newer joint called the Grain Station—an eccentric bar within an open-beamed old building directly across from campus, at 2004 Central Avenue SE—serves beer and bratwurst to thirsty students avoiding the classroom.

2. ISLA ÁNGEL DE LA GUARDA, SEA OF CORTEZ

Mexico's wild coastline along the Sea of Cortez was one of Abbey's favorite places to roam over the years, and this remote desert isle ("Archangel Island" in English) plays a memorable part in Abbey's nonfiction writing. He published articles about this isolated paradise in *Backpacker* and *Outside* magazines, with the lasting version of his Isla Ángel de la Guarda adventure appearing in *Abbey's Road*. A love-triangle novel set on the desert island was never finished, and maybe never started, but he did pitch the idea to his publisher in New York.

3. DEATH VALLEY AND ASH MEADOWS

Abbey's best-known book, *Desert Solitaire*, is mostly set within Utah's slickrock desert, specifically Arches National Monument. But much of the book was written and revised at a bordello in Ash

Meadows, Nevada—that's according to Abbey himself, in the preface to *Beyond the Wall*, and confirmed by those who crossed his path at the time.

Now a national wildlife refuge just east of Death Valley National Park, Ash Meadows Sky Ranch was a brothel and motel in the mid-1960s, when Abbey was working as a school bus driver, taking kids back and forth between Furnace Creek and Shoshone. While the students sat in class, Abbey worked on his manuscript within the cool dark confines of the Ash Meadows brothel in this High Desert oasis thirteen miles northeast of Death Valley Junction.

"The final chapters were composed in the corner of a bar serving as a legal house of prostitution at Ash Meadows, Nevada," Abbey writes in *Beyond the Wall*, "where I waited each day with my little yellow school bus (I was the driver) to pick up the children from Shoshone High School for transfer to the village of Furnace Creek in Death Valley. While waiting, I scribbled."

With editing assistance from a "sweet young sexual therapist named Alicia," Abbey completed the *Solitaire* manuscript and sent it off to his publisher, "book rate."

He wasn't the only artist taking refuge around Death Valley: Also in 1967, a fateful flat tire led a New York ballerina named Marta Becket to Death Valley Junction, where the Pacific Borax Company had constructed a community hall and hotel back in the 1920s. Becket fell in love with the place and remained there for the rest of her life. As for Ash

Meadows Sky Ranch, the ruins are now surrounded by a wildlife refuge managed by the U.S. Fish & Wildlife Service. This arrangement saved the sublime oasis and its many rare species from being developed into a twenty-thousand-home suburb northwest of Pahrump.

Abbey's beloved brothel and makeshift writing office of 1966–67 just happened to be built upon one of the most biologically diverse spots in the world. The Ash Meadows Amargosa pupfish, which lives only in the ancient glacial waters that spring forth here, is one of the twenty species of animals and plants found nowhere else.

4. WOLF HOLE, ARIZONA

Long before he claimed residency in the rural Arizona settlement called Oracle, Abbey signed off with "Wolf Hole, Arizona"—a patch of sagebrush on the Arizona strip, hours of grueling dirt roads north of the Grand Canyon. But a poetic lie is as good as the truth, which is how the real Wolf Hole has lured many Abbey aficionados to this wisp of a ghost town so ghostly that it's hard to find a trace of it.

Somewhat spoiling Abbey's prank was the creation of Parashant National Monument, in January 2000. Now you can bounce past Wolf Hole on the way to this immense, wild plateau leading to the most remote part of the Grand Canyon's North Rim. That all of this is just a few hours south of I-15, between the twin atrocities of Mesquite and St. George, makes it even more delightful.

5. ARCHES NATIONAL PARK AND MOAB, UTAH

Desert Solitaire is the primary reason so many hikers and bikers and other economically useful travelers venture to this relatively small park, far from the tourist resorts of Bryce and Zion. But there's no Abbey memorial, and you'll find scant mention of the seasonal ranger who became the best publicity Arches ever had. Ask about Abbey's old trailer at the visitor center and you'll likely be given some bureaucratic hogwash about how the site cannot be divulged because of various regulations and subsections of Interior Department policy.

Government is a stack of paper. But government employees are just people, mostly good people, and some of them are as interested in the Abbey legend as any sunburnt college junior with a backpack full of Abbey books. The longtime Arches ranger Lee Ferguson even revealed the location of Abbey's "little tin government house trailer" in a recent guidebook, *National Geographic's Secrets of the National Parks*.

"It was located right by the picnic tables on Willow Springs Road," Ferguson writes. Driving into the park, watch for the Balanced Rock parking area on the right—and then go left. Take the other. Your electronic map will show "BLM 378." And just five hundred feet up this good dirt road, you'll find a pleasant picnic area behind a clump of junipers.

Before you go, look up a short video essay by Abbey and the television producer Ned Judge called "I Loved It . . . I Loved It All." In this delightful feature intended for an NBC newsmagazine show in the 1980s, Abbey speeds around Arches in a red convertible and points to the spot where he claims his trailer once stood: another four hundred feet northwest on Willow Springs Road, beneath a road-maintenance gravel pile. Whether it's another Abbey prank or the secret truth, go take a look. You're close enough. "When I die, if I live that long, I'd like to be buried under this pile of gravel here," Abbey says.

6. EL PINACATE Y GRAN DESIERTO DE ALTAR BIOSPHERE RESERVE, SONORA

Running parallel to Cabeza Prieta National Wildlife Refuge, this immense Mexican wilderness preserve holds some of the wildest and least-visited desert in North America. Chock-full of critters, including herds of Sonoran pronghorn and desert bighorn, El Pinacate ranges from cholla-saguaro woodland to volcanic moonscapes. Abbey rambled all around here, camping on the Sea of Cortez and exploring the old volcanoes with fellow National Park Service rangers. Thanks to the kind of anti-immigration hysteria that Abbey encouraged during his final years, just getting down here today is a depressing journey through an overbudgeted yet inept police state. But don't hold it against the eighteen-year-old American military kids stuck out here to "help the Border Patrol." They're just trying to make a living like everyone (and everything) else in this hot, harsh, and remarkable stretch of desert.

7. BIG BEND NATIONAL PARK, TEXAS

This majestic country, along the Mexican border but also deep in the southwesternmost pocket of Texas, is prime Chihuahuan Desert—the most biologically diverse desert in the world, according to the World Wildlife Fund.

Abbey occasionally visited Big Bend when he was living up the road in Albuquerque during the late 1940s and early 1950s. Big Bend is the setting of his cautionary tale about a "preliminary honeymoon" in *Abbey's Road*. According to the unreliable narrator, a disastrous trip to Big Bend—disastrous for his future father-in-law's new car, anyway—ended the marriage before it officially began. As Abbey was married five times, including to both of his fiancées from the 1950s, this story can be safely filed in the "Wishful Thinking" folder.

Abbey rafted the Rio Grande through Big Bend National Park in 1974, with no less a river guide than his friend Ken Sleight, the man who inspired the "Seldom Seen Smith" character in the novel *The Monkey Wrench Gang*.

8. TUCSON, ARIZONA

This was home for much of Abbey's life, with enough traffic and land rapists and tract-home developers to fuel a thousand diatribes. It's also a beautiful town, especially in the foothills. Abbey occasionally expressed contentment with being here, but often escaped to fire lookouts or the cooler slickrock country in summertime. He found himself comfortably chained to the University of Arizona, where several of his wives attended college and he eventually became a full professor, teaching in the master's writing program.

His outlaw's grave site in the desert wilderness is legend, but it was in his writing cabin behind a modest little 1950s house on the western edge of Tucson that Edward Abbey died, on March 14, 1989. His final home base, "Ft. Llatikcuf," sits on 4.55 acres now surrounded by housing tracts, off Sweetwater Drive. Esperero Canyon, where he owned a beloved stone house in the early 1970s, is now full of gated communities and golf resorts.

Abbey's papers (along with Charles Bukowski's) are in the University of Arizona Special Collections Library. As for Abbey's beloved "Big A" burger-and-beer joint, just off campus, it closed in 1987. There's a Taco Bell there now, at 1818 E. Speedway Boulevard.

9. AZTEC PEAK, ARIZONA

One of the seasonal fire-lookout jobs Abbey used as a regular escape was at Aztec Peak, about a three-hour drive north of Tucson, in Tonto National Forest. It's easy enough to find, at the end of National Forest Road 487, which changes names three times before it ends again, in a ravine about a mile to the west. The perfect hideout.

10. CABEZA PRIETA NATIONAL WILDLIFE REFUGE, ARIZONA

We come to the end of our ramble here in the wild Sonoran Desert, where Abbey's road also ends. After his death in March 1989, at age sixty-two, his dear friends Jack Loeffler and Doug Peacock packed him in an ice-filled body bag and headed for Cabeza Prieta; his father-in-law, Tom Cartwright, and brother-in-law, Steve Prescott, also joined this last Abbey camping trip. His gravestone is a rock marked "No Comment." Whether it's in the refuge or Organ Pipe or the gunnery range or just south of the border is known only to Abbey's closest friends and family.

SCARY STORIES AROUND THE CAMPFIRE

We have been telling campfire stories since the early days of our haunted species, when humans first figured out how to start a fire for cooking, for warmth, for light. Wildfires are terrifying and destructive. Campfires are something altogether different—unless a careless campfire triggers a wildfire, as is sometimes the case in our dry western lands, charring hundreds or thousands of acres, destroying century-old trees, pushing burned and thirsty wildlife into suburbs and onto highways, the daytime sky turned black, the walls of unstoppable flame, the ground scorched, the boulders and logs and mud and bones ready to roll down in great waves of catastrophe with the next rain. If it ever rains again.

Anyway, campfires are nice. It's pleasant to sit in a circle around the tamed little inferno, the blue and red and yellow tongues of fire flickering over and around the split wood. A drink in hand, the immense, quiet darkness behind you. It's where stories have always been told, the dancing flames hypnotizing both listener and storyteller. If the tale is frightening, everybody moves in closer, toward the light and the warmth. If it's boring in a good-natured way, you think about getting in the sleeping bag, turning in for the night, hopefully after a long day of hiking or fishing or taking pictures of cactus and lizards and wildflowers.

Religion began at the campfire, along with fairy tales and other sorts of fables and philosophy and fiction. It's good for the soul, to sit around with friends and strangers, figuring out how to approach life, where to find the deer, the best way through the mountain pass, which caves are filled with hideous hell-monsters, etc.

We don't spend enough nights around a campfire, in our world today. There are cleaner and more efficient ways to make light and warmth for our 7.8 billion people, such as a couple of solar panels on the roof. But we rarely gather around the solar panels or the LED fixtures to tell stories. We need to go outside for that, a beach or a campground or a little spot well off the trail out in the backcountry, really any place with a relatively dark sky and crisp air.

Wherever you live in the world, there are weird and wonderful tales about that place, almost always about the *edges* of that civilization: the abandoned mines and munitions factories, the shadowy woods, the fierce deserts, the bizarre formations of rock. People *see* things out here, out there, if they come with the right kind of eyes. If their internal antennae are tuned to the right frequency.

You might have encounters with gods and monsters, angels and demons, lights in the sky and growling entities around the tent. Not everybody, of course. If everybody saw Yucca Man and burning bushes and hovering black triangles, they would be mundane, like cable-television programs about dragons and media and political corruption.

We are a fractured and confused people in this strange century, and most of what once connected us to a place—knowledge of the land and the animals, origins of the regional beasts and abominations, shared rituals and traditions—has been lost or taken away. We are strangers in our own land.

But we don't have to be like that. With a bit of pleasant effort, we can know our local critters and plants, our legends and lore, and we can experience things more directly.

We can gather around the campfire. It's the best place to be when night has fallen on the desert.

And night is the most interesting part of the day in the desert, and very much so in the summer, when most wild animals are at rest in cool underground burrows. Humans, horseflies, ravens, roadrunners, and the occasional brain-fried coyote—those are the kinds of animals foolish enough to be out in the heat of the day.

A seemingly barren desert landscape, like the Kelso sand dunes in Mojave National Preserve, comes to life in the night: fringe-toed lizards and kangaroo rats, sidewinders and kit foxes. Take a walk through a Joshua tree woodland at dusk then return in the morning. You'll find whole highways of tracks: herds of mule deer and bighorns; the wandering, heavier prints of coyotes and mountain lions; the rope-shaped tracks of rattlers and gopher snakes.

Look in a dry wash and try to find a sandy spot *without* tracks, especially the tiny marks left by beetles, centipedes, and scorpions.

Now, I want to tell you about the most *desert* of desert animals, a life-form so insane it hardly seems real: It prowls by night, it howls like a high-pitched wolf, and it eats mostly centipedes and scorpions. I'm talking about the fierce rodent we call the grasshopper mouse, about four inches of pure nocturnal terror, not including its long tail.

These New World killers don't just eat scorpions, they eat the stingers. They eat the stingers *first*. And the scorpion venom doesn't bother them. In fact, they get high from it. They love it.

Just a few years back, in 2013, a study found that the most potent scorpion venom, that of the tiny bark scorpion, was transubstantiated by the grasshopper mouse into a painkiller. The research paper, "Voltage-Gated Sodium Channel in Grasshopper Mice Defends Against Bark Scorpion Toxin," was published in the journal *Science*, written by Ashlee Rowe and her team at the University of Texas at Austin.

Other things come out at night, too. On a spring night in 2016, a man was driving southwest from Pahrump, Nevada, headed toward Twentynine Palms. He had planned to stay in Pahrump or Shoshone, but he hadn't made a reservation because he hadn't known every room in the area was booked for a footrace, a 120-

mile relay race of some kind, and almost all the runners were police. So he refilled his coffee at the truck stop and headed home, which wasn't really all that far, and it was a pleasant night for taking the Mojave back roads.

After crossing Route 66 and the railroad tracks, he was driving at a leisurely sixty-two miles per hour or so, on cruise control, because there are sometimes highway patrol cars hiding by the salt-evaporation ponds run by Amboy's National Chloride Company—Amboy was founded by salt miners on Bristol Dry Lake back in 1858, and that's the same sodium chloride we use to keep the ice off the roads in the Sierra—so he continued up the grade toward the Sheep Hole Mountains and Cleghorn Lakes Wilderness, nobody ahead and nobody behind, a clear night and a nearly full moon, and then in the rearview he saw headlights.

The headlights come racing up the grade, fourteen miles in ten minutes, and this driver is tailgating, and won't pass even though there's not another car anywhere in either direction.

So our driver taps the brakes a couple of times to show his displeasure, and, still blinded by this cretin's high beams, slows to forty-five . . . thirty-five . . . and finally, disgusted, comes to a complete stop in the road. And turns his head around just in time to watch the piercing white lights rapidly retreat miles down the grade, and then come to a sudden stop, and then blink off entirely.

The driver was still in that frame of mind so common to Americans behind the wheel, which is simmering road rage, and it was only as he crossed Wonder

Valley that the absolute weirdness of the situation settled in. There wasn't another *car* at all. The only thing he *saw* was a pair of bright lights that followed and harassed him between the salt ponds and the summit on Amboy Road. Even when he turned around to face the car that had stopped behind him in the southbound lane, he didn't see a *car*—just those infuriating lights, which retreated at a ridiculous speed and then simply blinked out. A car, it halfway occurred to him, would have probably turned around. Or passed him? Or the driver would've gotten out and blasted a hole through his head with a sawed-off shotgun, that's the kind of thing that's a legitimate concern when you encounter some unhinged nutjob in the middle of the night on an empty road in the Mojave Desert.

That very concern, in fact, was what killed off any ideas about driving back down the grade to see what, if anything, was now waiting for him, several miles away.

That whole tale is true, or at least that's how I remember it. I was the one planning to stay in Pahrump that night, because I was up there that day, hiking through the wildflowers. It was the end of the Death Valley superbloom in the spring of 2016, and even the tail end of that display was incredible and well worth the drive.

We classify and organize our memories, automatically. Think of your parents and you might think of the places where you grew up, holidays, tragedies, hopefully some joy. Think about different jobs you've had and you'll see the faces of the people you worked with, for good or ill.

I had put this particular memory into an automatically created folder titled "Encounters with Various Desert Creeps and Criminals." It's where you file stories like "A guy tries to get into your car while you're pumping gas in Ridgecrest," or "People in the motel room next to you in Victorville are apparently discussing burying a body," that kind of thing.

Until I did my periodic scanning of the new eyewitness accounts posted on the National UFO Reporting Center website, the Amboy Road lights remained "likely human" in origin. Having long had an interest in esoteric subjects, and having seen a number of bewildering sights in the desert sky, I like to hear about what other people are seeing, or think they've seen. And so this one caught my eye, reportedly having occurred at approximately 11:40 p.m., eastbound on Highway 79, just beyond the small mountain settlement of Warner Springs, near Anza-Borrego Desert State Park.

The summary was titled "Tailgating Vehicle Disappears." Here's what this witness reported:

> While traveling east on Highway 79, another vehicle came up from behind and began tailgating me at 65 mph. I slowed to 50 mph to express my dissatisfaction with this miscreant. That didn't work so slowed again to about 40 mph. Then the "headlights" from this vehicle just disappeared. I thought that the driver had foolishly shut them off, so I slowed to a near stop and carefully searched my rearview mirror. There was a moon, so I could see well. There was no vehicle and I

am certain that it did not leave the road, as this is cattle country with fencing coming all the way up to the shoulder. There is only one dirt driveway in this area, but I was not upon that. There are no trees or bushes along this road to hide a car. The vehicle did not pass nor turn around, it was just gone.

It just goes to show how a memory can have a whole new dimension when you classify it differently. Seeing someone else's account of such a similar oddball event presented as a *UFO report* made me wonder why I'd dismissed something so weird as just another dirtbag trying to get himself arrested, again.

Weird lights have harassed travelers on lonesome roads for thousands of years. People used to call them "spook lights" or "will o' the wisps." There are famous ghost lights in West Texas in the desert outside of Marfa, and in the Australian desert you can see the mysterious Min Min Lights, named for the old Hotel Min Min. In John Milton's time, the English called them friar's lanterns. And in the southwestern backcountry of our own era, some of us think of common human drivers with apparently magical abilities, while others go right to the UFO-reporting website. Scientists have studied some of these persistent lights, too, and have come up with possible solutions, including static electricity and geologic movements causing the formation of plasma balls that don't just hover but appear to act with intelligence, even malice.

The strange things that happen to us—especially

the strange things that happen to us in the quiet of the desert—seem ready for whatever explanation first comes to mind. There was a minor official in a minor province of the Roman Empire some years back, traveling with companions to Damascus, today the capital of war-torn Syria. Luke writes in the Acts of the Apostles, "As he neared Damascus on his journey, suddenly a light from heaven flashed around him. He fell to the ground."

A blinding light. One of those rare and purposeful beams of light that we are told strike certain individuals at key moments in their lives: Nikola Tesla as a child in the Balkans, Philip K. Dick in Fullerton, Bob Dylan in his bedroom in Malibu, Merle Haggard in a small plane over Point Conception, Joan of Arc's blinding visions, Saint Catherine receiving the stigmata from a dense beam of otherworldly light.

Saul had been busy trying to break up a new cult in Jerusalem that had attracted the local rabble, the same way the cops busted up Occupy Wall Street. It's what the boss always wants. Keep things calm. Root out the troublemakers. Law and order.

And we are told that Saul was on his way to Damascus to hunt down the remnants of the Jerusalem cult in the Syrian synagogues. Saul had never known the martyr these followers now called their Lord, but when his mind filled with an internal voice that seemed to be coming from the blinding beams of light on this desert highway, he suddenly believed it was the spirit of this street preacher executed by the empire. Saul converted to the new faith, then and there. Because he saw weird lights in the desert, the global religion he helped establish is still being practiced today, some two thousand years later. Saul would become known as the missionary Paul, who wrote the defining books and letters of Christianity, for millennia the defining philosophy of the Western world.

You never know what's going to happen on a lonesome desert highway.

PAHRANAGAT MAN: AREA 51'S ANCIENT MONSTER

Groom Lake is a smooth playa of hardened sand and minerals. When it rains, which it does every now and then, the former lake is briefly blessed with a sheen of shallow water that reflects the desert sky. When this occurs, the birds appear on these usually dry lakebeds, immense flocks of migrating ducks and geese and more exotic species that spot the temporary oasis from high above and settle in while the water lasts, which is not for long. Besides, this is a place of human disturbance. The playa here is for the testing of exotic aircraft, at unpredictable hours.

In the autumn of 1849, a wagon train of gold-rush pioneers led by Captain Jefferson Hunt camped at the dry lake. Hunt was Kentucky-born and had joined the Latter-Day Saints' cause at Nauvoo, Illinois. A high priest and proud polygamist, he had fled Illinois in the wake of Joseph Smith's murder at the hands of an anti-Mormon mob, and he earned his rank in the Mormon

Battalion before hiring himself out as a trail guide to the forty-niners arriving daily in Salt Lake City, itself still a rough camp that had been settled by the Mormons only two years earlier.

The Donner Party had passed through in 1846, its scattered and weary families attempting an October crossing of the Sierra Nevada. Of the eighty-seven souls together at Utah's Wasatch Mountains, only forty-eight made it over the mountains. Gruesome tales of their misfortunes sold many newspapers the following spring and discouraged the meek.

A southern route that avoided the Sierra was the only choice once snow began falling. The dilemma at Groom Lake was that no one was familiar with the southern trail to the California gold fields, and only the Mormons had any experience with the desert.

Here the wagon train split up and wearying misadventures were suffered. The parties would mostly meet up again at the place they would name Death Valley. The name was an exaggeration. Only one of the Death Valley forty-niners perished there, and the Timbisha Shoshone have lived in the valley and surrounding forested mountains for a thousand years.

It is relatively easy to travel across the Great Basin and Mojave Desert today. People still die on the road, or die on day hikes a few miles from busy campgrounds, but it takes no special skill to survive the journey. Water is secured from faucets and convenience stores. It is unnecessary, unlike in Captain Hunt's time, to read the landscape, to correctly guess that Crystal Springs in the Pahranagat Valley would have at least a little water for themselves and their starving oxen.

Crystal Springs is now served by an automobile rest stop on Nevada's Highway 375. The pioneers would have seen strange figures upon the boulders here, haunting petroglyphs of weird entities looming over bighorn sheep, coyotes, and humans. If these confused forty-niners went up Mount Irish in search of water and forage for their beasts of burden, more of these eerie figures would have been visible, pecked into the boulders hundreds and thousands of years before the gold rush.

This distinctive rock art, accessed today by that modern highway, is found only within Lincoln County, Nevada. There are two main types of mystery figures here: a decorated rectangle known to anthropologists as the Pahranagat Patterned Body Anthropomorph, or PBA, and the humanoid entity simply called Pahranagat Man. One prominent example of the latter makes it clear that this figure is male.

What "P-man" represents to you will depend largely upon your age and the culture you grew up within. Those who spent a lot of time watching television at the turn of the century might see Bender, the alcoholic robot from the animated series *Futurama*. The devout may see the Devil of their nightmares, with its long, bony fingers and hollow, expressionless eyes. Unlike many ghostly, floating figures of ancient rock art, Pahranagat Man usually has humanoid limbs: legs, feet, jointed arms, hands with fingers and thumbs. And if you are familiar with the folklore of extraterrestrial alien pilots visiting the Earth in spaceships, these figures on the desert rocks look like space monsters. Aliens.

No one is sure how old they are, or who made them. It is notoriously difficult to carbon-date ancient rock art, as petroglyphs in particular don't rely upon organic paint or pigment, and radiocarbon dating is unhelpful without the presence of carbon. But educated guesses can be made, based on the relative age of nearby artifacts such as rubbish piles and ancient campsites. And at least some of the Pahranagat Valley figures and patterns are pictographs, made with charcoal or blood or plants or whatever else was available. Petroglyphs, which get their color from exposing the rock surface beneath the natural "desert varnish" that often covers weather-exposed boulders, tend to outlive their painted companions.

This is why various experts will claim the Pahranagat rock art dates back more than thirty-five hundred years, or five thousand years, or maybe only five hundred years. Crude stick figures of Spanish horsemen argue for later dates, but the large and elaborate figures of the entities share nothing but a canvas with those postcolonial scribbles. What is known is that peo-

ple have lived in the Pahranagat Valley for at least twelve thousand years.

Those first inhabitants were the Patayan and Anasazi, and most archaeologists believe these early Pueblo peoples created the astonishing rock-art figures of southern Nevada. Modern Shoshone, Piute, Mojave, Ute, and even Comanche—who split from the Shoshone and made the mostly dry White River their western territorial boundary—have occupied the territory since the arrival of the Spanish.

Figures of sprightly bighorn sheep and human families of parents and children require little interpretation. But the immense gap in time, culture, language, and mythology makes it impossible for either archaeologists or today's native peoples to accurately "read" the abstract and symbolic rock art left by the prehistoric tribes. What should we make of the striking images left behind by ancient nomads in the Mount Irish Wilderness, such as the insectlike humanoid standing next to what looks to modern eyes like a giant sombrero or a 1950s flying saucer? What do we make of the human figure cowering behind his shield?

In the paranoid peacetime gap between World War II and the Cold War, the UFO era was born. And it began in the western United States, over the course of a few early summer days in 1947, with the pilot Kenneth Arnold's sighting of a fleet of boomerang-shaped silvery craft over Mount Rainier, followed by hundreds of sightings by credible witnesses. By July 8 of that year—only two weeks after Arnold's sighting—Roswell Army Air Field in New Mexico announced that the "many rumors regarding the flying disc became a reality" when a crashed disc was retrieved from a local rancher's rangeland. The U.S. military would spend the next half century walking back that press release.

Groom Lake began its military life as a World War II aircraft-gunnery range, and the isolation of the dry lake made it the choice of California's aerospace industry to test incredible new surveillance aircraft for the escalating Cold War. Lockheed was working on a fantastic high-altitude spy plane. The secrecy around the project meant that Edwards Air Force Base, in the Western Mojave, was too visible, too close to Southern California civilization. The Lockheed plant in Palmdale had the same problem: too many people around and above.

And so Lockheed's Kelly Johnson took part in an aerial reconnaissance in 1955. With fifty sites under consideration, Johnson took a "hunting trip" by plane and was shown Groom Lake, surrounded by high, barren mountains and buffered by the immense Nevada Test Site.

"Man alive," said Johnson, the U-2 spy plane's chief designer. "We looked at that lake, and we all looked at each other. It was another Edwards! So we wheeled around, landed on that lake, taxied up to one end of it. It was a perfect natural landing field."

This top-secret extension of Edwards AFB would be

kept quiet. Even the name was secret, and was only barely acknowledged by the CIA in 2013. There are competing theories about where "Area 51" came from; Johnson named the site "Paradise Ranch." When the CIA referred to the site, internally, it was either Groom Lake or Homey Airfield.

The high-altitude testing of the U-2 and SR-71 Blackbird caused people in and around Las Vegas to believe they'd seen UFOs—which, technically, is exactly what they had witnessed—but the alien lore surrounding this airfield was a distinct product of the 1980s.

As the Clark County population swelled into fresh desert suburbs and the new residents began enjoying the clear night skies, there were many rumors about the base beyond Nellis and the Nevada Test Site. Private pilots were sternly warned away from the area, and employees arrived by a secret airline that flew out of McCarran Airport, right off the Las Vegas Strip. There was already a paranormal late-night talk show on local radio, pre–Art Bell, and there was a wealthy hotel developer in Las Vegas named Robert Bigelow who had a deep personal interest in the UFO mystery. A number of flying saucer conspiracists were already obsessed with the eastern boundary of Area 51, including John Lear, son of the Lear Jet founder and reportedly a CIA contract pilot. It was John Lear who brought a KLAS-TV reporter named George Knapp into the flying-disc subculture, in 1987.

Some two years later, Robert Lazar appeared on the KLAS-TV news to claim he'd worked on reverse-engineered flying saucers. Lazar's voice was electronically altered, and his face was in shadow, and he was originally identified only as "Dennis." Lear was by now a friend of both Lazar and Knapp. Lear vouched for Lazar, and claimed they had both witnessed UFOs in "test flights" over Area 51.

Lazar's Area 51 stories sounded goofy to real physicists, and his personal life was a mess of running away from bad debt and knocking around the Southwest, from his community college in the Los Angeles suburbs to New Mexico and next to Las Vegas, land of third chances. And then there was the bigamy, and moving into the dead wife's house with the new wife, and the conviction for running an illegal brothel in Clark County. Prostitution is allowed in some Nevada counties, including neighboring Nye, but these backroads bordellos are far from the lucrative tourist trade in Vegas and Reno.

It didn't matter that Lazar had puffed up his résumé to include advanced degrees from MIT *and* Caltech, even though his academic records are limited to some classes at Pierce Community College, in the San Fernando Valley. It didn't much matter that the one professor Lazar could name from MIT or Caltech turned out to be a Pierce teacher. Bob Lazar delivered the story, and the story hit a nerve. For thirty years after he told his incredible tale on local television—that he had worked for a few weeks on recovered flying saucers at an unknown sub-base called S-4—Lazar mostly lived in obscurity. The mythology didn't need him. It just needed a new Roswell.

Area 51 became a meme of the first kind, a deep mythology that burrowed into the collective consciousness and never really left. *The X-Files* and *Independence Day* brought the paranoid tales to prime-time television and summer blockbusters. Video games, pop music, comic books, and the early Internet message boards elaborated the theology. Like Roswell before it, Nevada's Area 51 became a collective dreamland of extraterrestrial secrets.

Pilots had been referring to the top-secret air force base at Groom Lake as "Dreamland" for years. Strange things were seen over this easternmost extension of Edwards Air Force Base, wonders in the sky. Some of these aerial oddities were later revealed as SR-71 Blackbird and U-2 spy planes. Some were Russian jet fighters stolen from Soviet airfields. And some remain unexplained: lights dancing in the sky, things that hovered with no visible or audible means of propulsion, sinister black triangles making 180-degree turns and shooting off like meteors.

Nevada is mostly federal land, and Area 51 is part of a vast, secret complex that includes the nation's nuclear testing grounds at Yucca Flat, Nellis Air Force Range, and the heavily litigated nuclear waste dump within Yucca Mountain.

On the northeast side of Area 51, where Highway 375 skirts the base's buffer zone, tourists have been coming for a quarter century to drink alien-labeled bottles of beer at the Little A'Le'Inn and take some pictures by the rural mailbox that marks a dirt road leading to the edge of the base. There's the Alien Research Center down the road in Hiko, too, with a giant metallic space alien standing sentry outside the souvenir shop.

The Nevada Commission on Tourism quickly recognized the value of the alien legends, and in 1996 the state highway was renamed the Extraterrestrial Highway. Actors from the movie *Independence Day* and the television show *Star Trek: The Next Generation* attended the opening ceremony with then-governor Bob Miller. A cache of science fiction souvenirs went into a time capsule in Rachel, the contents of which will likely baffle archaeologists of the future as the Pahranagat Man figures baffle us today.

The UFO phenomenon is deeply weird and chaotic, like the subculture around it.

A close-range encounter shakes a person's very soul. During the 1997 Phoenix Lights event, people pulled over on the freeways, gazing up in astonishment and horror at mile-wide silent aircraft that appeared to be right on top of them. The sense that the government is lying about UFOs is hard to avoid when, as happened in Phoenix, the governor himself takes part in a staged charade meant to belittle the reality of what occurred. Arizona's governor at the time, Fife Symington, concealed his own up-close sighting on that otherworldly night of March 13, 1997, while mocking his constituents who were badly shaken from seeing the same phenomena. (Symington eventually admitted all, a decade later, on CNN. He remains convinced the craft he witnessed that night was "not of this world.")

There's a baffling strangeness to these events. They rarely make any practical sense. The laws of physics are routinely and absurdly broken. And yet they are objectively real to the witnesses, regardless of what's really behind the flying saucers and black triangles and other bizarre apparitions that haunt our skies and our social media. Military pilots chase them. Commercial pilots nervously report them. Millions of people around the world see unidentified aerial phenomena every year.

UFOs are socially disruptive. The effects are unpredictable. An obvious meme or a science fiction story can be taken at face value. Absurdities and counterintelligence operations become reality. Jokes, hoaxes, lies, con men, and chaos are not bugs in the UFO operating system. They're a feature.

Around the world, but most vividly in the indigenous culture of the American Southwest, the trickster wreaks havoc for good or ill or just for the hell of it, right here in our everyday world. The trickster isn't condemned to rule an underworld like some lesser god of the Levant, because the trickster is an equal among gods. A lot of credible people have looked at Lazar's story and rationally concluded that he made it up. He was, after all, convicted of felony pandering within a few months of his making wild claims about working on alien saucers. And since childhood he had courted local publicity, first for his rocket-powered bicycle, later for a rocket-powered Honda hatchback. He could've remained "Dennis" forever, but he wanted his name on the tale. And for thirty years, he has mostly stuck to the details of his flying saucer story.

By 2019, only the small and graying contingent of late-twentieth-century UFO researchers were familiar with the story, and they had mostly dismissed it. Jeremy Corbell, a tattooed and bearded independent filmmaker who lives part-time near Pioneertown, in the California desert, is fascinated by Lazar. Corbell has made a trio of feature-length documentaries about the UFO world, but his Lazar movie blasted right out of the flying saucer cult and became a full-on pop culture phenomenon. *Bob Lazar: Area 51 and Flying Saucers* spent much of the summer of 2019 as the number-one documentary on Netflix, right there on the home screen for millions of subscribers worldwide. It was already doing well when the monstrously popular podcaster Joe Rogan brought Corbell and Lazar on his show.

Three decades later, people are again thinking about that mysterious desert military installation 150 miles north of Las Vegas.

UFOs are an inescapable and crucial part of desert history and culture: Roswell, Groom Lake, the UFO contactee George Van Tassel's Integratron, Gram Parsons and Keith Richards watching for flying saucers from a barber's chair they dragged up a mountain in Joshua Tree. Corbell introduced himself to me, at the High Desert restaurant La Copine, and said we needed to know each other. Adventures followed.

On a mild spring day in the Mojave, a hundred miles north of Las Vegas, Corbell and I were in the back seat of a Toyota 4Runner headed straight up a mountain dirt road just beyond Area 51. George Knapp and his KLAS photographer Matt Adams were up front. They had all joined me for an archaeological field trip. I was seeking Pahranagat Man, in person. The distinctive figure is found only in the ancient rock art of Lincoln County, around Groom Lake. This entity being so similar to the popular conception of "space aliens" supposedly kept at Area 51, I thought it might be worthwhile to gaze upon these remote petroglyph panels and contemplate the ridiculous synchronicity.

A full day of traveling, hiking, and ascending steep dirt tracks resulted in about an hour of mesmerized viewing at just two of the half dozen major sites in Lincoln County. We had nearly given up in the Mount Irish Wilderness when Matt Adams made one more pass in the 4Runner and brought us to the treasures of Shaman's Knob, which we had already passed several times.

This rock art can be difficult to find, and that's on purpose. Whether under the administration of a tribe, a military base, a national park, or the federal Bureau of Land Management, petroglyphs and pictographs usually take a little effort to reach. Any archaeological treasure too close to paved roads and bored rednecks is at risk of casual destruction. Even remote petroglyphs attract professional crews of raiders, who arrive by helicopter and remove boulders or whole "panels" of petroglyphs from the sides of canyons and mountains. The famed Sunburst Petroglyph outside of Ridgecrest, California, was stolen in this way just a few days before the massive Ridgecrest-Trona quakes of July 2019.

Of the great historical waves of sightings, the most dramatic can predict future Earth technology, like the aerodynamic marvels seen up and down California during the mystery airship flap of 1896. Within twenty years of that hysteria, such airships were ferrying passengers across the skies, but they could never maneuver like those bizarre airships over San Francisco and Sacramento, with their impossibly bright spotlights and ability to vanish.

The black triangles predicted the shape and color, if not the performance, of the B-2 Stealth Bomber, which lacks the ability to hover silently over shocked motorists on a desert highway before shooting off into the atmosphere without producing so much as a breeze. I have witnessed one of these silent craft low over the desert floor on the 395 in the Owens Valley, as have thousands of other California drivers who will never forget that particular road trip. There is a great mystery to it all, and the Hollywood conception of space aliens does not do it justice.

For those who have yet to experience the eerie silence and heavy wonder of a close-up encounter, the mythology is enough. Matty Roberts, a twenty-year-old engineering student in Bakersfield, came up with a viral online joke about storming Area 51 to "see them aliens" and attracted nearly four million "likes" on Facebook alone.

Jeremy Corbell suspected that his own documentary about Area 51's secrets had triggered the meme, and soon he had tracked Roberts down and proposed, along with the owner of the Alien Research Center on the E.T. Highway, a massive UFO-culture festival on September 20, 2019, the random date chosen by Roberts for his #StormArea51.

There was a lot of hype, and a couple of Dutch YouTubers even managed to get arrested and deported before the event as they clumsily attempted to raid Area 51 on their own. The festival itself was a dud, having split into separate amateurish events in Rachel and elsewhere. Media people outnumbered the few attendees. Even the UFO faithful will tell you that Area 51 has long received too much attention to be the home of any great alien conspiracy. If the Grays and the Reptilians dwell within some U.S. facility, it is likely nowhere near the garish signs for the Extraterrestrial Highway and the nearby desert metropolis of Las Vegas.

While alien life remains unproven in Lincoln

County, there was a significant arrival from outer space in these same Mojave mountains. It was the Alamo bolide impact, some 367 million years ago. The geologic evidence stretches from one end of the Extraterrestrial Highway to the other.

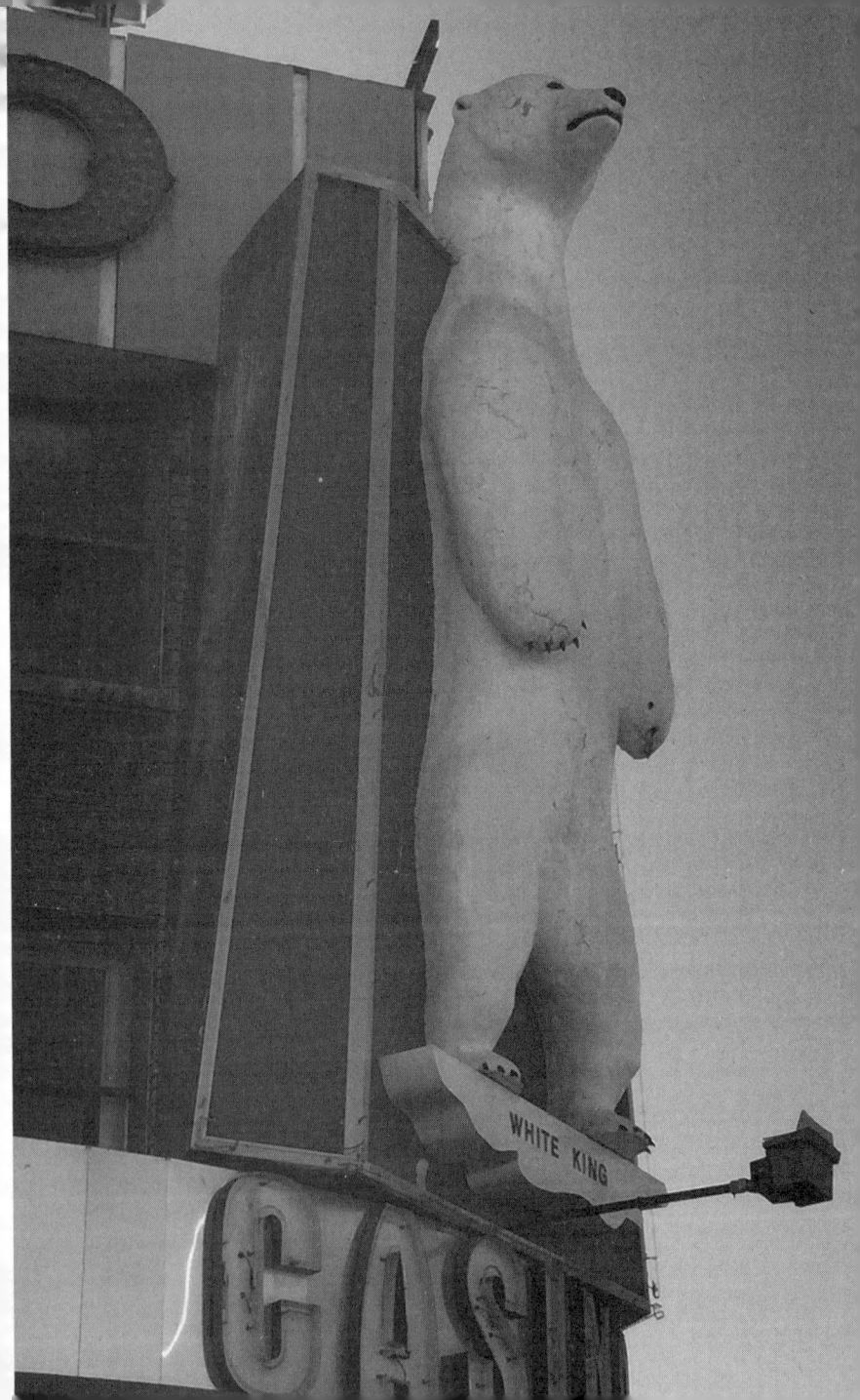

COWBOYS AND POETS

Poetry rests fairly low on my list of concerns, and I've never been terribly fond of cowboys, real or imagined. Yet here I was at the Cowboy Poetry Gathering in Elko, Nevada—more specifically, at the bar of Luciano's Restaurant on Silver Street in the old downtown.

To my right sat a tall, bearded southerner who said he was working around the West as a welder. He had, for example, welded the immense flaming iron octopus that was reportedly a recent favorite at Burning Man. The barmaid, a young woman born and raised in Elko, had seen this flaming octopus at Burning Man. She was impressed.

A local rancher was deep in conversation with a young couple traveling through town. The subject was wine: varietals, the soil and sun of Napa County in California, etc. Then a pair of very image-conscious cowboys burst in, talking loud enough for everyone to hear. They settled at the bar next to me and ordered drinks and dinner—we were all dining at the bar, because it's sociable and also because every table was full on this Saturday night.

The main cowboy had a perfectly trimmed goatee and a new hat and one of those long duster coats like you see in old movies or karaoke country videos. His sidekick was dressed more plainly, befitting the sidekick's role.

Pretty soon the cowboys had taken over the conversation with a lot of talk about horses and fences, and I said with some suspicion, "Where are you guys from?"

"New York," the main cowboy whispered.

Never be ashamed of where you're from—it's not your fault. Nobody loves the Southwest like us transplants from the Northeast or the Deep South. Ask Edward Abbey, born and raised in the Appalachian town of Indiana, Pennsylvania, twenty-eight miles south of Punxsutawney.

Some years ago I hired a couple of guys to fix up the fence so my dog couldn't leap over it every time a coyote or bobcat strolled by, and one of these guys was kind enough to mention that the new gate I'd requested was going to open "right onto a cactus."

I followed him to the spot, where he pointed out the "cactus"—a seven-foot-tall Joshua tree.

"Let's move the gate over to the next post," I said. "Where are you guys from, anyway?"

"Born and raised right down the road," he said, pointing to the village of Joshua Tree.

The best thing I saw in Elko was outside the Denny's overlooking the interstate: a gleaming row of silver-and-red Tesla electric-car-charging stations. Driving lonesome two-lanes across the deserts is one of the great joys of life, a close second to walking alone in the wilderness. But the driving comes with some guilt in the early years of the twenty-first century.

Ed Abbey has a much-quoted bit in *Desert Solitaire* about how you can't see anything from a car because you need to slither around the rocks like a gopher snake or whatever, but Ed Abbey loved his daylong desert drives so much he measured them by the six-pack. And now our half-robotic gasoline-powered cars can measure the miles by carbon emissions.

Those fancy new electric-car-charging stations—especially the ones connected to rooftop solar and battery banks right there where the juice is needed—have the ability to put the fun back in driving for the sheer hell of it. Tehachapi to Tonopah? Charge up the pickup.

A DAY HIKE TO HELL AND BACK

A popular campground within Joshua Tree National Park is Black Rock Canyon, at the end of a dead-end road in Yucca Valley. It wasn't always a national park campground. It used to be called Jellystone Park, complete with statues of Yogi Bear and twentieth-century amusements such as a miniature golf course. A company had franchised these places here and there, all over America. Eventually the old Jellystone Park of the High Desert, opened in 1971, was sold to the National Park Service, and now you'll have a hard time finding any signs of Yogi Bear on the property.

There are trails that go up to Eureka Peak and all the way over to Keys View, and there's a very interesting trail that winds through a low canyon to the spring, where flocks of pinyon jays live in the shady piñon trees there.

In September 2010, a man named Edward Rosenthal drove up from Los Angeles to Black Rock Canyon for a day hike. Because of the higher elevation, it's much more pleasant than much of Joshua Tree or Twentynine Palms in the summer.

Ed Rosenthal was in a very good mood. Then a fifty-seven-year-old commercial broker, he had just made a big real estate deal, involving the last surviving Clifton's Cafeteria in downtown Los Angeles.

Clifton's has been a landmark for nearly a century, the first restaurant having opened in 1931, just as the Great Depression was settling in. Charles Bukowski used to eat there, as a young man, and he writes in his book *Ham on Rye* that the original owner allowed poor people to "pay what you can," so that nobody went hungry.

"It was owned by some nice old rich man," Bukowski wrote. "A very unusual person." Clifford and Nelda Clinton ran their business on Christian ethics and later retired to run a charity dedicated to feeding the hungry, "Meals for Millions."

Science fiction writers loved the two downtown locations, as did members of various UFO and alien-contact clubs in Los Angeles. Ray Bradbury was a regular, and so were Robert Heinlein and L. Ron Hubbard and Forrest Ackerman, all part of a loose-knit gang of sci-fi writers who had weekly meetings there among the taxidermy animals and water features.

The place was a Disneyland before its time, with some sections of the multistory cafeterias made to look like treehouses or jungle encampments.

It was the decrepit old Clifton's Brookdale that Ed Rosenthal had just sold to a nightclub operator, and Rosenthal was happy, happy enough to drive out to his favorite place, Black Rock Canyon, just about two hours by car from downtown Los Angeles, if the traffic's right.

But it was a bad time of year for hiking, even at the higher altitudes. It was monsoon season, muggy and humid, the kind of weather that makes you want to give up and die. He walked and walked and he got lost and confused, trying to retrace his steps in the midday sun, and then it was the next day, and the next day. For six impossible days he was lost. He kept to what little shade he could find, during the worst of it, but he was turned around completely.

The search-and-rescue helicopter went back and forth over the northwestern corner of the national park, and neighbors on the trails in the morning and evening would look for signs of this man. But they were looking in the wrong place.

He wound up all the way down by Desert Hot Springs, near the southwestern boundary of the national park. It was hot as hell down there and he finally gave up. Writing on his sun hat with a ballpoint pen from his pocket, he scribbled a will, and said goodbye to his wife and friends and family. He still had his wits, right at the end.

But he didn't die. In fact, he was found alive, just after he finished scribbling his last will and testament on the brim of his hat. The rescue team got him to the Hi-Desert Medical Center and he survived that, too. He was tired and dehydrated, but otherwise free of serious injury.

Ed Rosenthal was a rare case: He vanished and was

found alive in a desert wilderness. He lived to tell the tale.

Every summer, tourists die in the desert national parks and monuments: Joshua Tree, Death Valley, Mojave National Preserve, Mojave Trails. They'll be walking around with their families and suddenly they have trouble breathing and need to take a little rest. And then the pulse stops.

Sometimes they're middle-aged hikers like Ed Rosenthal, in good shape and fairly familiar with the area. Sometimes they're young and healthy Europeans on holiday. Sometimes they're regular Americans trying to see some nature, regular Americans in regular lousy health, staggering around in the blinding sun, wondering why their cell phones won't work.

Park rangers in the desert southwest have a name for a particular way people die these days: death by GPS. Tourists follow their car's navigation system, ignoring whatever common sense might otherwise prevent them from driving a rental car down a rough dirt road that leads them farther and farther away from water or help. And then they run out of gas or get stuck in the sand, and then they try to walk back, in the 120-degree Death Valley summer heat, or a "hot enough" 104-degree afternoon in Joshua Tree.

The summer after Rosenthal's brush with death, a European couple perished out by Eagle Mountain. Guus Van Hove, forty-four, and Helena Nuellett, thirty-eight, had come for a summer vacation to see the Mojave because they loved that U2 record, *The Joshua*

Tree—even though the record was made in Ireland, nowhere near the desert, and even though the long-dead Joshua tree photographed for the record's cover was up in Darwin, near Death Valley, most of a day's drive from Joshua Tree. Their rental car, a Dodge Charger, got stuck in the sand and they tried to walk out.

Late summer is a cursed time of year for the desert visitor. Every August, right on time, people start disappearing. It happens too often in national parks and national forests. People just disappear.

Sometimes it's planned. You can hardly blame anybody for wanting to drop all this banal madness, student loans and credit cards and car payments and health insurance premiums and insulting jobs that can be taken away at any moment. Why not just fake your death in the desert and start fresh somewhere?

Usually, it's not planned at all. It's a preventable accident, an avoidable misfortune. Ed Rosenthal knew more than most about hiking these deserts, and he still nearly died out there, walking distance from a busy campground.

PHILOSOPHY ON THE ROCKS

What did Mojave pioneers do with their spare time in the days before satellite TV and cell phones? They thought about the big questions, about humanity and nature and the point of it all.

And in the peculiar case of an immigrant from Sweden named John Samuelson, these thoughts were carved into a series of split boulders around his homestead in Lost Horse Valley—now a popular part of Joshua Tree National Park.

It was 1926 when Samuelson showed up at Bill Keys's ranch looking for work. Hard labor awaited on Keys's gold claims.

By 1927, the Swede had settled down with his wife, Margaret, on a nice patch of desert in the hills, a few miles northwest of Quail Springs. When he wasn't mining his own claims or tending to the daily needs of a desert homesteader, Samuelson worked on his commonsense nature-based philosophy, which he forever preserved on a group of eight boulders, give or take some smaller rocks with lesser markings.

The Perry Mason creator and pulp author Erle Stanley Gardner was just a desert-loving Los Angeles attorney with a dream of becoming a crime-story writer when he met Samuelson at the springs by chance during a backcountry outing. Gardner served up a couple of cocktails and paid twenty dollars for the rights to Samuelson's ridiculous and likely fictional life story.

Featuring tragedy and magic and shipwrecks and movie-style escapes from Cape Town gangsters and African tribes, Gardner's action-adventure tale of the Swedish desert rat was published by *Argosy* magazine and later found its way into a racist pamphlet that used the unlikely story as propaganda for the pseudoscience of "eugenics."

But Samuelson's life had much more drama to come: Having lost his mining claims in court, he headed to Los Angeles, feeling robbed of the desert home he so loved, where his mind could linger on moral philosophy rather than his fellow man.

One grim honky-tonk night in 1929, a dance-hall brawl in Compton left two men dead. The accused killer, John Samuelson, was pronounced insane and sent to the state prison hospital in Mendocino. He escaped a year later.

Nobody ever saw him in California again, as he managed to disappear into the Pacific Northwest and worked for more than two decades at logging camps, on the edge of civilization.

Bill Keys tells of receiving a letter from his former employee and neighbor in 1954, a quarter century after the dance-hall killings. Samuelson made clear his longing for his desert homestead, but knew he could never return without facing justice.

A logging accident took John Samuelson's life a year later, and he might have been forgotten if not for the curious messages branded in the rocks around his old home. The land remained private over the generations, an island, or "inholding," within Joshua Tree National Park, left off the National Park Service hiking-trail maps, yet known to those who seek out-of-the-way spots.

In the summer of 2017, this homestead was purchased by the Mojave Desert Land Trust and is on its way to becoming part of the national park. More than 160 such inholdings have been acquired and protected by the Joshua Tree–based land trust.

To visit these curious relics, go to the Quail Springs picnic area and walk the dry wash for 2.5 miles west-northwest. It's a fairly easy early morning hike, 5 miles total. Carry water and tell somebody where you're going!

THE MURDER KING OF WESTERN SWING

The music called western swing was born in the desert southwest. The people did not come together peacefully, but their music did: Spanish guitars, German accordions, African drums, the song styles of Tin Pan Alley and Hollywood cowboy movies. New Orleans jazz. Memphis blues. Ancient folk songs from the British Isles and romantic ballads from the wide-open deserts of Mexico and the ranchos of Alta California.

The music was made for dancing—first at "ranch dances" in Texas and New Mexico and across the old Southwest. People would come from miles around for parties that could last for many nights, musicians crowded into a corner of the living room, partners swinging through the kitchen and hallways, kids gathered in the doorways, barbecue smoking outside, wagons and horses and maybe even a few automobiles circled around the ranch house.

If they were good, the musicians could work a circuit of hundreds of miles around the sparsely populated American west, traveling with guitars and violins, whole families of performers playing festivals and wedding parties, in matching suits or rodeo-style uniforms when available. It's music for celebration. Fiddle and guitar, the more the merrier. The violin had come to the New World with the conquistadors, as it later came to Virginia with the English and to Nova Scotia with the French. In Spanish America, it was joined with the Spanish guitar, a Renaissance-era four-stringed instrument with a fretboard and tuning pegs.

Guitar is not a Spanish word; it's a hybrid Persian and Sanskrit word, with "tar" being the Sanskrit word for "string" and "guit" being our modern American pronunciation of the old Persian version of the Sanskrit word for "four," as in four strings, an update of the stringed instrument beloved by the Moors and the French troubadours, brought to Spain with the Arab conquest. And it all got mixed up in Texas a hundred years ago, mixed up with any rhythm or style or instrument or melody that caught the musicians' ear.

Bob Wills heard a lot of this ranch music when he was growing up in Texas, and he played it, too. Bob Wills soaked it up. He was born to a family of farmers and fiddlers, at a time when such musical

families—Mexican, Anglo, Polish—were crossing the dusty roads of the Southwest headed to another fandango, another rodeo, another feast day, another wedding or funeral or roundup. Records were new, radio was new, and the only sure way to make a dollar was to show up and perform, like it is again for musicians today. Make the people dance.

As English-speaking Americans moved west—whether pioneers or Civil War refugees or those chasing gold or silver or empire, land to graze cattle, crude oil and aerospace jobs, seeking adventure or escaping trouble—the language of the music adapted. What had been exclusively Spanish and Mexican music became what we call western music: cowboy songs accompanied by the Spanish guitar, groups with two or three or maybe a half dozen violins, piano if there was one available, horns if there were horn players. Old fiddle tunes from England were introduced, mixed with tunes from Mexico and Africa and universal lamentations.

All kinds of music exploded into being in the early twentieth century: jazz played by small combos with banjos and brass, country blues in Mississippi, ragtime in the cities, hillbilly music recorded for the first time in Bristol, Tennessee. Well, what if you put a classical orchestra in a ballroom with a jazz beat? Why not add a Hawaiian steel guitar, and why not rig up some speakers to amplify the Spanish acoustic? Everybody saw the potential in those accordions and harmonicas from the Habsburg Empire. Percussion led to a jazz drum set, loud and clear. People wanted to dance!

In Texas, this was all cooking up into something that would be called western swing. Today it's known as the official music of the state of Texas, to the point that it can be hard to imagine this music existing outside of Texas and Oklahoma and New Mexico. But it did. Western swing was born in Texas, but it grew up in California. It was biggest in the Golden State, and was the biggest music in California for decades. It was what you did on Saturday night. It ruled the live radio broadcast and the barn dance, the barroom, the fairground, and the Saturday matinees packed with kids and grown-ups.

Bob Wills and Milton Brown were especially interested in a New Orleans two-beat that kept people on the dance floor. This pair, Wills on the fiddle and Milton singing, had improvised together on "St. Louis Blues" back in 1930, at a house dance in Fort Worth. And right there, they knew they had something, something different. They formed a couple of groups together, each one drawing bigger crowds, playing to more people through the miracle of radio broadcasts, known as far as that clear-channel signal would reach as the Light Crust Doughboys. Then there was an argument about money and Milton Brown flew the coop, forming Milton Brown and his Musical Brownies, which was the biggest thing in Texas swing until 1936, when Milton crashed his car, likely from falling asleep on another long Texas drive between performances. He died a week later. All the dance bands were swinging now, and they called it swing, too. Bands that could swing would ride a two- or a four-beat or maybe something fancier, as long as the people were dancing. The players took turns soloing, improvising, as in New Orleans jazz. People started buying a new kind of shoe: dancing shoes.

Bob Wills and Milton Brown had remained friends after they split up, and Wills based his new, bigger group on the Musical Brownies. With Milton lost to the highway, Wills picked up some extra musicians, too. Bob Wills and the Texas Playboys proved right away they were bigger than Texas, as they set up shop in Tulsa and took over a low-ceilinged ballroom and the best spots on local radio, where you could really hear the smooth, rich vocals of Tommy Duncan, just a beautiful thing to hear with Bob Wills's "hot dance band." Tommy Duncan might be the best male singer in the history of American popular music, able to do standards and jazz, hillbilly and swing, low-down blues, novelty and cowboy songs, and he always made it sound effortless and romantic. Western swing is romantic music: love and loss, the frontier and the range, saloon and jailhouse, twin fiddles harmonizing behind the story song. Listen to something like "Bubbles in My Beer" and be amazed how, as Frank Sinatra would do in the 1950s, Tommy Duncan makes a sad-sack barstool tune sound dignified, if resigned. And all the while, Bob Wills is making wisecracks and asides. It all sounds too nutty to work, but it worked well, and still sounds great today.

But Bob Wills had begun looking west. By the 1930s, the Dust Bowl and the Depression and the general restless nature of America meant people were moving west in droves, settling in Seattle and San Diego, Portland and Phoenix, Bakersfield and Modesto, but especially Los Angeles, which had given up its sleepy reputation as an old Spanish cow town.

Donnell Clyde Cooley was born in Pack Saddle Creek, Oklahoma, in 1910. Of Cherokee and English blood, he was born to the fiddle, like his father and grandfather. Playing music wasn't much of a living, even though it was too deep in his heart to ignore. His whole sharecropper family headed for Oregon, where he attended the Chemawa Indian School and took cello and violin lessons. And then down to Modesto, where he started playing the bars and staying up late playing poker, even though he still had to work the fields at dawn. That's where Donnell Clyde picked up his card skills and picked up a nickname at a poker game: Spade. Spade Cooley.

Now, Spade Cooley could play the fiddle, and maybe he was better than Bob Wills and maybe he wasn't. But he was good, and he was something to see. He got a job in Los Angeles, in either 1934 or 1937. Nobody was keeping notes at the time. Spade Cooley was a nobody, and he washed up in L.A. with all of six cents in his pocket, along with a new wife and baby. Things were starting to cook in Los Angeles, new saloons and ballrooms and radio stations, great mobs of humanity out on the street, looking for fun, looking for relief from a world of insanity. Sailors, soldiers, Okies, nurses and waitresses, factory workers and truck drivers. Los Angeles was bulging with restless people in these years of Depression that became years of world war in a Pacific port city. People were even going out to the seaside now, ignoring the old idea that living by the beach was bad for your health. Honky-tonk neighborhoods replaced coastal wetlands, great piers and docks were constructed, gambling and booze ships bobbed in the waters just out of reach of the feds.

Spade met a western musician named Len Slye, who had some success with a group called the Sons of the Pioneers. You could hardly tell Spade and Slye apart.

The Sons of the Pioneers hired Spade Cooley, as his friend Len Slye was heading off to become something new: an American entertainment icon named Roy Rogers. And because Spade was about Roy Rogers's size and had Roy Rogers's eyes and was good on a horse, he worked as Rogers's double in the cowboy movies. Cooley wouldn't have to go back to the cotton fields of Modesto after all. Everything was starting to happen.

Just as the world fell in love with California cowboy music, that particular variety of western-themed pop songs with Mexican guitars and fiddles, the best players were already considering themselves jazz musicians, a new kind of urbane jazz musician, now as often white as black, but mostly playing for Okies. These players could read music, whether from a classical education or learned by necessity. Movies and records needed great orchestras and small combos, musicians able to play any style, able to sound like the court musicians at an

Arabian Nights harem or a German symphony or whatever the song or the motion picture called for, and this you could hear in music that was relentless in adapting various styles. Cosmopolitan, you could call it, but the players and the audiences took on the movie-costume style of the western cowboy and cowgirl, with embroidered suits and clean white hats and pointy Mexican boots. Nobody wanted to be called an Okie, even if that's what they were, but everybody liked to dress up as a California cowboy. And California cowboys gathered at the beach.

With those grand piers at Venice and Santa Monica and San Diego came enormous, elaborate ballrooms. A Texan transplant and Los Angeles deejay called Foreman Phillips was known far and wide for his *Western Hit Parade* broadcast, and he knew there was an audience for something bigger than honky-tonks. With so many talented and movie-famous musicians in Los Angeles, Phillips rightly figured that he could pack 'em into these seaside ballrooms. Spade Cooley and his orchestra proved the gamble, when something like seven thousand people showed up to dance at Cooley's show on the Santa Monica pier, and the whole thing was shaking to the point that management feared the pier would collapse into the ocean.

What Bob Wills realized was that people in California were crazy for his kind of music—the musical style he originated along with the late Milton Brown—but he wasn't there yet to play it. On the strength of the beautiful and romantic song Wills called "San Antonio

Rose," Irving Berlin paid a publishing advance and encouraged Wills to put words to the fiddle tune. He did, with help from the band, and the 1940 Columbia recording of "New San Antonio Rose" is perfection, a beautiful and instantly memorable melody played in the swing-band style of the day, with Tommy Duncan's smooth delivery, that mix of sophistication and jukebox heartbreak, an idealized and cleaned-up version of the ranch dance, now featuring an eighteen-piece orchestra that Wills called the "finest jazzmen you ever heard," a band he built to do anything, and to do it with style. Everybody was playing "San Antonio Rose" in the 1940s, and by the 1950s it was a beloved part of the American songbook. Bing Crosby did a great vocal on his cut, just a year after Bob Wills put out his new version with lyrics. Patsy Cline, Gene Autry, Patti Page, Ray Price, Les Paul and Mary Ford, Lawrence Welk and his Dixieland Boys—everybody did "San Antonio Rose." The crowds at the pier ballrooms demanded it. And the jazzmen knew it was great stuff, too. With Wills and his group still based in Tulsa, the magazine *Metronome* published the kind of review any jazz musician would cherish, but it was about a group far from the bandstands of New York and Los Angeles.

And this group was the biggest seller on Columbia Records' roster.

Bob and an abbreviated version of his group came out west to make a motion picture, costarring with Tex Ritter. People loved it. Most of his listeners had never seen Bob Wills and his Texas Playboys, even if only five were there for the first movie. A year later, in 1941, Wills and the group did their first Hollywood recording session, and it must've been illuminating to see the big city falling over itself to welcome these cowboy musicians who expertly performed jazz and blues and swing. When they played the California ballroom circuit for the first time, in 1942, Wills realized he had boxed himself into Texas and Oklahoma because he was scared he couldn't make it in New York and Hollywood. He was incorrect.

Thousands filled the dance floors. Hundreds were turned away nightly. With a talented writer named Cindy Walker churning out memorable songs for Bob Wills and the Playboys' cowboy musicals of 1940 to 1946, the style was now visual, too. Realism in westerns would have to wait. People wanted fun, hot music and slick costumes. And they didn't seem to mind that Bob's "cowboy band" had a bigger horn section than Glenn Miller's orchestra. It was music that offered sublime beauty with a hit-parade sensibility, breathtaking musical skill with sweet and sometimes hokey sentiment. It was music with a big heart.

He could have stayed in Hollywood, but at times Bob Wills lacked the confidence, felt himself an impostor, felt he "fit" best in Oklahoma, playing that Southwest circuit. Wills took the band back to Tulsa, where complications awaited: ex-wives and new wives, contracts and finances, and especially the draft board, which would chop up and separate the Texas Playboys at the height of their musical powers. Milton Brown was the father of western swing, when people remembered him at all. And Bob Wills was the king. But in the absence of the rightful king, Spade Cooley claimed the title for himself, out in Hollywood. It was his to take. In January 1945, Spade Cooley and his Western Band, featuring the great Tex Williams on vocals, released their signature song, a neat little swinging taunt called "Shame on You." The lyrics are Spade's, it is said. The music may or may not have been composed with his bandmate Smokey Rogers. Spade grinned when he played it, but it still sounds too heavy for the lighthearted arrangement.

Shame, shame on you
Shame, shame on you
Two can play your little game
You'll find out who was to blame
Durn your hide
Shame on you

"Hide your face," went Spade Cooley's trademark hit. "Shame on You."

You hear a name like "Smokey Rogers" and you think, Now, who was that guy? Well, Smokey Rogers was from Tennessee, and by the mid-forties he was an important part of Cooley's western orchestra, and he was a successful songwriter, too. He wrote "Spanish Fandango" with Bob Wills! Eventually he and Tex Williams split off from Spade, because Spade was becoming difficult. Smokey and Tex formed the Western Caravan, and then Smokey took some Capitol Records money and took over the Bostonia Ballroom, the pride of El Cajon, California, and the southernmost stop on the western swing ballroom circuit. Everybody played the Bostonia, from the Texas Playboys to Hank Williams, Patsy Cline, Johnny Cash and the Tennessee Two, and Marty Robbins, and for years Smokey had his Bostonia barn dance program on channel 8 in San Diego. There was a kid in north San Diego County who played mandolin, and his local bluegrass group opened for some of the big country acts at the Bostonia. One day the kid looked up and Tex Williams himself was listening to the picking, praising the teenager's mandolin skills. It meant a lot to young Chris Hillman, who would shortly go on to form the Byrds, and then the Flying Burrito Brothers, and it turned out the Burritos' pedal steel guitar player, Sneaky Pete Kleinow, had been Smokey's steel player at the Bostonia, and that's where he picked up the "Sneaky" part of his name, which always unnerved Chris Hillman, wondering what Pete had done to earn such a moniker.

Everybody loved Spade Cooley. His appeal does not translate today, for whatever reasons. We are usually stuck in one mode of witnessing time, because we generally see from only one direction in time. Now to "back then." Present to past. We cannot reliably see the future.

And sometimes a person of note is forgotten not because of the quality of their work, or the relative success and notability of their art, or because their entire civilization or culture was lost, or because of a later effort to steal their glory or copy their invention, but because of a kind of psychic curating performed by the collective consciousness. A primitive but pure form of democracy, the quiet action of history's will. Today we call it cancel culture, but it has always been part of human society.

Spade Cooley was famous not for a few months or years but for decades. He transcended his era's limitations of race and class and jumped from medium to medium: live performance, live radio, hit records, hit movies, and for many years, a hit TV show. Like Lawrence Welk's, the North Dakota accordionist and bandleader who had a lasting career with his "sweet" champagne style, Spade Cooley's career aged with his audience. Like his friend Roy Rogers, Cooley had not only jumped from hillbilly music to movies and TV, he had also become a businessman. And like both Roy Rogers and Lawrence Welk, Spade Cooley would invest his money and celebrity on real estate ventures.

He was a fair and honest business partner, it is said.

Cooley was known for saying "It's a deal, son!" He was an easy man to work with, generous yet clever. After all, he got his nickname from an incredible three-in-a-row run of all-spades flushes at the poker table. Spade Cooley and his western orchestra played regular ballroom engagements to five thousand or eight thousand or twelve thousand wildly enthusiastic Southern Californians, year after year, through some of the liveliest times in America. He was top draw in a swinging town like Los Angeles, where you could hear the top jazz acts all over town. Central Avenue, on both sides of Vernon, had the wildest jazz and R&B acts in the country, in the world. Charles Mingus and Max Roach. Dexter Gordon and Woody Herman, Johnny Otis and Etta James. Can you imagine walking down Central Avenue in the early 1940s? All the cowboy music, the big bands, the pop vocalists, the symphonies, and none of them could draw a crowd like Spade Cooley. He packed them in at the Venice Pier Ballroom until he could fit no more. Then he leased the biggest dance hall in town, the Santa Monica Ballroom. Packed 'em in there, too.

Funny thing about Lawrence Welk: His first big hit was a cover of "Shame on You," the Spade Cooley hit. Red Foley sang the vocal on Welk's version. And Welk's version actually topped Spade Cooley's on the charts, number 4 to Cooley's number 5. You maybe wouldn't expect Lawrence Welk to keep showing up in a story like this, but Spade Cooley's later orchestra and television persona had far more in common with Lawrence Welk's bubble-machine elevator music than the hot improvised dance jazz made by Bob Wills and the Texas Playboys.

Los Angeles was the wildest music scene in the world in that wild time. Orchestral composers who had recently fled Nazi Germany—fled for their lives—were now writing movie soundtracks and arranging string sections on pop records. L.A. had southern bluesmen. Gospel singers. Mariachi bands and pachuco boogie, the style of Chicano jump blues born in L.A. The Blasters cofounder Dave Alvin, from the L.A. Basin town of Downey, wrote a song called "American Music" that could've fairly been named "L.A. Music":

> *We got the Louisiana boogie and the delta blues*
> *We got country, swing, and rockabilly, too*
> *We got jazz, country-western and Chicago blues*
> *It's the greatest music that you ever knew . . .*

But by the 1950s, Los Angeles music was most widely heard in the form of national music shows such as *Western Ranch Party*, which was broadcast across the country from Compton. West Coast western swing was making its on-and-off transition to West Coast rockabilly and the Bakersfield sound, and it remained popular even as the ballroom scene came to a sudden end. Maybe it was television or maybe it was the weight of a sudden 30 percent federal tax on nightclubs with dancing. Max Roach said that's what killed public dancing, "the real story" behind the sudden end of busy nightclubs full of happy people dancing to live music.

"Club owners and promoters couldn't afford the combined city and state government taxes," Roach said. It's one of the very interesting asides in one of the better histories of country music in California, *Workin' Man Blues* by Gerald Haslam—a book endorsed by Dave Alvin. While we're talking books, let's mention *San Antonio Rose*, an academic biography of Bob Wills, by Charles R. Townsend. (And if you're building up a library on American music, then you will want the greatest book on country music ever written, from 1977, by the recently departed Nick Tosches. It's simply called *Country: The Biggest Music in America*.)

Well, the cops and the chamber of commerce and the board of decency didn't want nightclubs around, anyway. The ballrooms survived this purge for a time. But the weekend dances couldn't survive television, and the baby boom, and the spread of the suburbs, and the tearing up of the city's great streetcar system that could take you to the pier and back again, no matter how much you'd been drinking.

Spade Cooley moved easily to television. His ballroom shows were really variety shows, with special guests from all over the entertainment world. On Spade's KTLA broadcast, *The Hoffman Hayride*, you could see hillbilly sibling acts or a rising star, and you could watch big headliners like Frank Sinatra as Spade's guest performer. The music itself was professional and very carefully arranged, with a few eccentric elements, such as dual accordions, along with the same instrumentation and sheet-music-reading players as you might see in any big-city ballroom band. By 1950, Spade Cooley's recorded music displayed this smooth and slick style to such a degree that it began to lose its association with hillbilly and western music altogether. While he remained a local star in the biggest local TV market around, and while he was both wealthy and famous, you don't hear much about Spade Cooley in the country music history of the 1950s. The hits stopped and did not return. His star vocalists moved on to their own western-style orchestras. Like Prince in his later career, Spade Cooley tried gimmicks such as all-female backing bands. But by the mid-1950s, rock 'n' roll and that explosive variety of Los Angeles rockabilly left the older generation clinging to the "sweet style."

Lawrence Welk took Spade Cooley's crown on local television. By 1958, Spade was mostly retired from performance and pursuing his other business interests. It seemed natural that Gene Autry and Roy Rogers should expand from white-hat singers to smiling middle-aged businessmen, as natural as Cal Worthington selling used cars with his cowboy hat and his dog, Spot. As natural as a cowboy-costumed television presenter named Ronald Reagan winning the governor's office, as would happen a decade later.

In fact, Ronald Reagan—Governor Ronald Reagan—

plays a small part in this tale, a part that Spade Cooley didn't live to learn about, because he died just beforehand.

In 1961, Spade Cooley was living in the desert. The Mojave Desert. He had a beautiful ranch house built on his property in Willow Springs, the far western edge of the Mojave, that corner of the Mojave under the jurisdiction of Kern County, up against the Tehachapis. Spade Cooley had very big business cooking up there. With Disneyland and Knott's Berry Farm drawing huge crowds in a southland hungry for entertainment, Spade had begun work on his own great theme park, a great theme park built upon the Mojave Desert, to be called Water Wonderland, near his Willow Springs home. Oh, it would be something else: golf courses and lakes and water slides and restaurants and thrill rides and a huge custom ballroom for huge dances. According to the papers, seventeen states were clamoring for a Roy Rogers Frontier Town theme park.

Well, Spade would have his theme park, too. If only he could focus.

Spade Cooley was having a difficult time of concentrating on the work at hand. It was his wife—his second wife. Ella Mae. He discovered her, as they say, and then he fell for her, and then he married her.

While Spade Cooley lived a nightlife common to honky-tonk musicians and tomcats, he remained married to Ella Mae. They raised a family together. As long as Ella Mae ignored his wandering, things seemed to be all right. There are tales of Spade Cooley's management office writing checks to his many one-night stands and side girls. The checks were for abortions. Maybe Spade Cooley could've become president after all, one day.

He was not bothered by his own infidelities. Ella Mae was his worry. What did she do while he was working or otherwise occupied in Los Angeles? Roy Rogers lived not far away, on a big deluxe horse ranch in Apple Valley, just past Victorville. And while Spade and Roy were friends and sometime business partners, lately Spade had gotten the idea that Roy had a thing for Ella Mae.

That would be trouble enough, but through a combination of rumor and fantasy, Spade Cooley decided that Ella Mae was part of Roy Rogers's secret sex cult. A free-love kind of thing, the sort of stuff that most people associate with a later era. But this was a Hollywood crowd, and Spade was convinced. He got himself real low down, and when he got down like that, he drank and drank until a beast emerged, and then he was Mr. Hyde. His friends and fellow musicians said he just dropped the guise of that fiddle-playing bandleader, the charming and generous Dr. Jekyll. Spade Cooley worked himself into a long, long rage. He worked himself into a rage as he drove up to the desert, up to Willow Springs, stewing over Ella Mae, what she might be doing behind his back, what she might be doing with

Roy Rogers and Dale Evans and some kind of horse-ranch free-love sex cult. People did get weird out in the desert. Still do.

Cooley's best-known songs, despite the smooth and orchestrated style, are full of menace and jealousy and prison. "Detour" is some kind of frantic nonsense about ignoring a detour sign and winding up in prison for years. Like everything Spade recorded, it sounds both cartoonish and slick, but it's the story of a wound-too-tight nutjob, verse after verse of numbing violence and insanity. Tex Williams does the vocal on this one, too, with Spade singing harmony on the chorus. As with most Spade Cooley songs, the blame is external. The detour sign is the problem, not the lunatic who plows through a road-closed warning and then commits so many unmentioned additional crimes that the judge gives him five years.

The 1945 hit "Troubled over You" has a sprightly opening, very Disney-cartoon soundtrack, with those increasingly prominent dual accordions and a syrupy string section. The story is the usual one for Spade: The woman cannot be trusted. The man is troubled over her, and also furious that when he whistles at other women on the street, his "honeybee" is angry. He just can't trust her.

"Shame on You" had long served as his signature song, performed countless times at ballrooms and on television and radio. It's an ugly lyric. It's as demeaning and complaining as a Billy Joel lyric, when you think about it. The woman will pay, pay for her lies. She took his car and his money. Tried to lie when he got wise. And then there's a hokey little bit of cowboy-movie dialogue, "Durn your hide."

Spade Cooley was going to durn Ella Mae's hide. He would take his time, make sure it hurt. Make sure she knew that two could play her little game, whatever the game was. Spade Cooley had so many reckless affairs that he was paying Hollywood doctors for abortions in the double digits. His manager, Bobbi Bennett, had gotten used to cutting those checks. For decades now, Spade Cooley had kept it together, just enough. Looking ahead to the nation we would become in time, it's easy to imagine Spade Cooley transitioning to the political stage. He was an exceedingly bad person, but he was rich in money and real estate, and he was famous from the teevee.

But the events of April 3, 1961, ensured that Spade Cooley's fame would forever turn to infamy. Fame is indifferent, part magic and part horse manure. Should you cross a certain line, you'll still be a person of note, but now the crowd is only there to delight in your fall. For a vain and paranoid and psychopathic man, the hard switch from beloved star to celebrity criminal must be the closest thing he felt to shame.

Spade Cooley would later claim a lot of stuff that didn't add up. He talked to Kern County detectives at the Mojave substation, on tape, for over an hour. He had a good defense, later, in what was called Bakersfield's Trial of the Century. Most of his claims, about

Ella Mae falling in the shower, about how he only pulled out some of her hair, about how she apparently admitted to both an affair with a UCLA professor in Los Angeles and being an enthusiastic participant in a Roy Rogers free-love sex cult on the same ranch property where the famous white horse Trigger enjoyed the finest stables money could buy, about how she had affairs with the two men Spade simultaneously insisted were exclusively homosexual. Most of the claims weren't possible to prove or disprove, really. Because by the time Spade Cooley took Ella Mae to the hospital in Tehachapi, she was no longer in a position to offer her side of the story.

The cause of death, ultimately, was that her heart was crushed, by direct assault to the victim's chest. Spade Cooley stomped Ella Mae to death, slowly. He didn't durn her hide, he burned it—burned her flesh with cigarettes, knocked her unconscious, and then waited, swallowing pills and gulping booze, until she came to just enough for the torture to continue. And then he got hold of his fourteen-year-old daughter, Melody, and locked her in the house. Kept her right there. And these are the words Spade Cooley told his daughter about her mother, bleeding on the floor: "You're going to watch me kill her."

One thing you'll find in this world is that the most evil people are unhealthily obsessed with police and law enforcement, not justice but raw power. Cooley loved being around the cops. He played any benefit they asked him to play, whether in L.A. or out in the desert. When his Kern County jailers realized they had the famous Spade Cooley as an inmate, he was given the run of the joint. He ate meals with the deputies and guards in their comfortable cafeteria. He wandered freely, his cell unlocked. He played music for jailer and jailed alike, and they overlooked the fact that he'd recently beaten and tortured his wife to death. There was blood all over the bed and the shower and just all over, really. And that was after he called his manager to drive up and help him out of a bind, and after a nurse was called to clean up the corpse a bit, after Ella Mae was long dead, naked and battered and bloodied and burnt. The trial lasted a month and was front-page news in California, San Francisco to San Diego.

Spade Cooley could've gotten off easier had he pled insanity. And for a moment that was his plan. But then they'd see his files, his psychological profile. Then they'd all know that Spade Cooley had come to the secret realization that he was, in fact, a homosexual. It was what he feared most, more than prison, more than execution. And so he sat there and smiled and lied and cried for the jury, oh, he prayed out loud for Ella Mae, for his children, for his dirty little sinner's soul. He was fifty years old when the verdict was delivered: life in prison, for the wrongs he'd done.

I've always wondered if the song "Life in Prison," the sad country classic by Kern County's own Merle Haggard, was about Spade Cooley. You might know the version by Chris Hillman and the rest of the country-western version of the Byrds, from the album *Sweetheart of the Rodeo*.

> *The jury found the verdict, first degree*
> *They swore I planned her death to be*
> . . . .
> *Insane with rage, I took my darling's life*
> *Because I loved her more than life*

Who knows. Once everybody involved is dead, you can't go back and ask them about it. Spade Cooley went to Vacaville, considered an easier state prison than the notorious San Quentin, the prison where young Merle Haggard found himself for three years. In fact, Haggard was paroled for his bungled and drunken attempted robbery just a month before Spade Cooley murdered Ella Mae. You can bet Haggard closely followed Bakersfield's Trial of the Century, the O.J. story of its time, just as a young and still-unknown Haggard returned home.

Spade Cooley served only eight years of his life sentence. Without any wives left to brutally murder, he was a model prisoner. And his fame still meant something in the law-enforcement world, the same law-enforcement world that was so furious about the Black Panthers and the hippies and the war protests. They still liked him just fine. By unanimous vote of the parole board, Spade Cooley would be a free man in 1970. And just to show how much the cops loved him, they let him out early, in 1969, to play a police benefit concert in Oakland. There was a special treat awaiting, too: After his performance, they were going to bring him back onstage to announce that Governor Ronald Reagan had approved Spade Cooley's complete pardon. Like none of it had ever happened.

Merle Haggard would get his own pardon from Reagan in 1972, having served hard time when he was just a poor kid in trouble, and then he'd gone on to a national career that far surpassed anything Cooley had done. Merle Haggard never forgot his time in prison, never forgot the poor people who made poor choices and always paid the price, never forgot how cops and guards protected their favorites. The music that Merle loved most was called western swing, so much so that in 1970 he recorded a tribute album to Bob Wills and the Texas Playboys, and he assembled all the aging, ailing Texas Playboys in California and made sure they were comfortable, made a certain dream come to life, a dream Bob Wills had that the whole band would retire together in the Central Valley, get together and play music in their golden years. Bob Wills had his demons, like most bandleaders, but he was a good man. A good man who was always a little overwhelmed by California.

Spade Cooley called himself the King of Western Swing. But the crown always belonged to Bob Wills. And after Cooley went to Vacaville there was never any more arguing about it. Bob Wills, as Waylon Jennings would sing, was still the king.

Anyway, Spade Cooley never learned of his pardon. He did not live to be paroled. Spade Cooley performed for the Alameda County Sheriff's Benefit and went backstage and sat down. His heart hadn't been good for a long time. He'd had a number of heart attacks, including a pretty good one after he was charged with murdering Ella Mae. But this was the big one. Spade Cooley fell over dead backstage in Oakland, California, on November 23, 1969. He was fifty-eight years old. Shame on him.

LA LLORONA IS COMING TO DROWN ALL THE CHILDREN

Hernán Cortés is remembered as the conqueror of Mexico, but it was his mistress Doña Marina who did the talking. It was she, a Nahua from the Mexican interior, who always accompanied the conquistador. She spoke with authority in Nahuatl, in Aztec, and then in Castilian Spanish. Enslaved and passed around neighboring cultures after her father's death, she was once called Malintzin. With another twenty slave women, she became a human gift to Cortés from the coastal Mayan people in the year 1519.

A striking beauty often depicted by the Aztecs as towering over Cortés himself, she is remembered for her linguistic ability and her symbolic role as mother of the first mestizo, fathered by the conqueror. And she is damned as the original *malinchista*, her namesake slur: a sellout, one who betrays her country for the approval of the Europeans, the white men.

The truth is five hundred years in the past now, impossible to see in the context of its faraway era. Modern historians say her diplomatic skills likely prevented more massacres of the kind that the Spaniards let loose upon the Aztec nobility, yet some historians now see her as the *real* conqueror of Mexico.

In the deep memory of the mixed and complex people born of Europe's thirst for empire, Malintzin is a spirit, too—a spirit that is part goddess, part guilt. She was, after all, named for the goddess of grass. But this was not the deity that would join her history in folklore: the heartsick mother searching the irrigation canals and rivers and lakes for her drowned children, for the children that she herself had murdered in rage and sorrow.

That entity is Chalchiuhtlicue, the Aztec water goddess . . . or is it Quilaztli, or Cihuacoatl, the snake goddess who abandoned her immortal son Mixcoatl at a lonely crossroads? Mythology and religion evolve with history, with culture, adapting and reusing the entities seen and heard on lonesome roads and waterways by night.

Such legends were not unique to Mexico. The Europeans brought their own: the Greek sorceress Medea and the Libyan princess Lamia, both compelled to kill their divine children and suffer the loss throughout eternity. Then there is the banshee of the Celtic tribes, known well by the conquistadors from Western Europe.

Folklorists and other historians will forever peck away at the origins of the mythology. The children of Mexico and the U.S. Southwest need not be burdened with the origin story—they know all they need to know when they hear the name "La Llorona." The Weeping Woman. The dark-haired weeping woman in the long white dress, her horrible wail breaking the silence of the rural night.

La Llorona is coming. Children mustn't linger outside after dark, unless they want to feel her cold, terrible hands wrap tightly around their little throats, silencing the young ones as she drags them into the water, enraged anew because these are not her children, either. She wails in the night, forever.

La Llorona is seen along the canals and the creeks, at the crossroads and along the highways, a figure in white, radiant yet only halfway here, halfway in our world and halfway in the other realm. She is often seen on the Old Spanish Trail through the Mojave Desert, the one we now call Route 66.

Dennis Dispenza went online to share his childhood memory of seeing, with his parents, La Llorona along the highway during the 1960s:

> We had an unusual encounter with a "Spanish Lady" on a road in the Mojave Desert east of Los Angeles, California, late one night in the early 1960s. She was very beautiful, dressed in a flowing white gown and headdress. She asked us if we could give her a ride into Los Angeles, as she had been left on the road after a quarrel. She seemed to have an odd glow to her. The experience was so peculiar that my parents finally de-

murred and drove off. My mother was very upset by the experience.

This spirit lady is also known to haunt the ghost town of Calico—now a tourist spot, outside of Barstow—and has been regularly encountered over the decades. The author Lorin Morgan-Richards claims to have seen the "White Lady" as the specter roamed the perimeter of Calico, and he describes this close encounter in his 2015 history of Celtic immigrants to the desert Southwest, *Welsh in the Old West*.

This wandering lady is not the friendly ghost who continues to reside in Lane's General Store. While the best-known photograph of the Calico pioneer and longtime shopkeeper Lucy Lane shows her in a long white dress, her ghost is a separate entity from that of the glowing Spanish Lady or White Lady of the Mojave. But Lucy Lane's wedding-day promenade down Calico's dusty streets in 1893 has fixed her in the place's memory: a woman in white, cheerfully walking in her wedding procession even as the hem of her long gown turned the color of desert sand.

Her presence is still felt within the old general store, which for many years served as the private residence of Lucy and her husband, the silver miner and longtime water superintendent for Calico, John Robert Lane.

When another local miner, Walter Knott, decided to purchase the faded mining town and turn it into a tourist attraction in the 1950s, Lucy Lane was long widowed and kept the general store as her home.

San Bernardino's *Sun-Telegram* reported in 1961 that the hordes of desert tourists forced Mrs. Lane "to put a 'private residence' sign on her front door or else be constantly interrupted."

Walter Knott saw so much potential in his ghost town that he constructed replicas of Calico's buildings for his Buena Park tourist attraction, Knott's Berry Farm. Calico itself he donated in 1966 to San Bernardino County, which maintains the old mining town as a historical park.

By then, Lucy Lane had finally retired to another iconic silver town, Virginia City, Nevada, where she died in 1967 at the age of ninety-one. While she had attended high school in Pomona, the desert always called her home, especially the harsh Mojave Desert around Calico, her primary home since arriving at the age of ten, in the year 1884.

The coal-mining towns of Utah's Carbon County have their own White Lady, with the usual mishmash of vague and disputed origins. What's not in dispute are the frequent appearances of a spectral woman in a long white gown, sometimes wailing and sometimes warning people to stay away from the crumbling mine tunnels around Spring Canyon, and especially in the ghost town of Latuda.

There are darker allegations, too: This ghost is said to lure people inside the dangerous mines, a legend connected to one of the worst coal-mine disasters in history. Exactly 199 men perished on May 1, 1900, when a spark ignited coal dust within the subterranean darkness of the Winter Quarters #4 mine. Some six decades later, the Ghost of Spring Canyon was linked to the explosion of the remaining mine structures, although a high school boy ultimately took the blame. Abandoned structures on the edge of western towns are favorite haunts of living teenagers, too.

Some of the richest tales of La Llorona come from Arizona, especially the ancient lands of Pinal and Maricopa Counties, home to the advanced agricultural civilizations of Sonoran Desert peoples that thrived for a thousand years, until the fifteenth century. When European colonists first explored the sun-blasted valleys of the Salt and Gila Rivers, more than a century after their abandonment, they found extensive networks of canals, intricate manufactured goods, and evidence of great ceremonial architecture such as the Casa Grande Ruins.

The writer Jason P. Woodbury, who grew up around Coolidge and Casa Grande, tells of La Llorona haunting the canals and farm roads of his youth. When the population of Arizona's "Valley of the Sun" began to thrive again in the twentieth century, those ancient canals were put back to use, feeding the cotton and alfalfa farms where the new Arizonans from Virginia and Kentucky and Illinois now toiled in the oppressive heat beneath a relentless sun. La Llorona claimed many young children attempting to cool off in the deep canals as their parents knelt in the cotton fields.

The memory of the land, of the irrigation and cultivation of this desert valley over two millennia, persists not only in the canals with their ancient pottery shards shoring up the levees, but in the collective memory of today's Arizonans. It is in and around the sprawl of Phoenix that La Llorona takes forms unknown in the rest of the Americas. It is here that she has made the difficult journey from ancient canals to modern plumbing. Within the restrooms of elementary schools and neighborhood parks of Phoenix and Glendale and Tucson, La Llorona haunts the sinks and bathroom mirrors. Here, instead of the "Bloody Mary" legend of Catholic schools, it is the Weeping Woman who appears in the darkened mirror. Invoke her at your own risk by chanting her cursed name.

Wherever Spanish and indigenous peoples mixed in the Americas, La Llorona thrives. She is part of the Halloween festivities at Florida theme parks and Día de los Muertos celebrations in old San Antonio, and she looms over San Francisco in Juana Alicia's 2004 mural in the Mission neighborhood, *La Llorona's Sacred Waters*.

On the Central Coast of California, the Chumash knew her from ancient times, and they called her Maxulaw—a panther-like creature with dark, leathery skin, who wails from the oak forests.

At the wild and magic place known as the Western Gate—today's Point Conception—the Chumash warily met this wailing gatekeeper from the Other World: La Llorona, the horrific messenger of death, the mournful phantom cursed to accompany souls between the dimensions, between realities. Listen for her, at the lonesome edge of town. Watch for her.

WONDER VALLEY

There are nine hundred people living in all of Wonder Valley. Seems like a lot of people. I've never seen more than about fifty people in Wonder Valley at one time, and that was at the Palms.

"This is a great place to run away from something," said Pastor Max Rossi, who heads one of the two churches serving Wonder Valley. "From a bad relationship, from debt, from bad parents, fears. People can run away into the desert and hide quite well."

That was a quote from *The Desert Sun*, the Palm Springs newspaper, a year or so back. I thought I might like this pastor. He sounded more aware of his surroundings than most people in that kind of work.

It was one of those articles that reporters write in hopes of getting a journalism award. So it had some semi-poetic parts, and then it was talking about the difficulties of living out here, and the list of usual minor discomforts like the 120-degree heat and the rattlesnakes wrapped up with "bobcats and vultures."

Now, I know a lot of people don't know much about

the desert and are scared of the whole idea, but "bobcats and vultures" are not usually on the danger list.

I have heard of bobcat mothers shrieking at people who got too close to wherever the babies are sleeping, which is sometimes in your backyard. There's a picture that goes around on the Internet every couple of years with somebody claiming they "found" a cat and it was so grumpy when they tried to wash it. And it's a bobcat. "Just a big grouch" is the text on one of these posts.

As for vultures, you are well out of danger before a vulture takes any interest in you.

There's a story people remember out here more than any story about philosophy or monsters because this story is about real estate, and better yet, it's about *free* real estate, the desert dream, the Kingdom of Heaven on Earth.

Well, free real estate is what the U.S. government offered to common Americans during the Depression, no bribes necessary, and all you had to do was go up to the Bureau of Land Management office and make your claim on one of the five-acre High Desert parcels made available by the Small Homestead Act of 1938.

Nearly a half-million acres of the Morongo Basin, including prime chunks of Pioneertown and Landers and Joshua Tree and Wonder Valley, were up for grabs. But only a third of those parcels went into private hands. The desert was wild and harder to get to back then. No water lines, no electricity, for many years no telephone, no television, no Netflix!

But the biggest hurdle was the requirement to build a cabin, a cabin that met the minimum specifications—the minimum viable product, as they say in Silicon Valley—a one-room, three-hundred-square-foot shack with an outhouse out back, that was the basic requirement. People with a little bit of money could get a prefab cabin fully installed on a slab for fourteen hundred dollars, and a little elbow grease and a truckload of lumber could go a long way toward building a jackrabbit homestead cabin yourself, especially if you brought a couple of buddies from work and a couple cases of Budweiser or Golden Grain, all iced up like the dickens. A cozy cinder block fireplace, pulling in Bob Wills and the Texas Playboys broadcasting live from Fresno on KMJ-AM, skies so full of stars that even on a moonless summer night you could walk outside barefoot and see well enough to step around the scorpions.

People made their claims, but many failed to "prove up," to prove they had built the required homestead cabin. These parcels went back to the government, back to protected desert land, available for public use, and hopefully not for abuse.

It's why you can sometimes find a Wonder Valley cabin today with maybe one neighbor and the other three parcels open BLM land. And on a nice winter's day, you can walk right out of your homesteader and up to Cleghorn Lakes, without ever crossing another person's private property, without ever risking a backside full of birdshot from an aggrieved neighbor.

The most famous homestead flunky was none other than Ronald Reagan, who got a taste for the desert while shooting *Death Valley Days*, and who took the trouble to file his claim. But he failed to prove up, he never built his homestead shack, and the "playground of the presidents" thankfully remained down in Rancho Mirage and Palm Desert, leaving the High Desert to the people least likely to start a nuclear war, even if they wanted to.

WHEN EISENHOWER MET THE SPACE ALIENS

When the health resorts of Palm Springs became tennis clubs and golf resorts, the sunny winter resort began attracting American presidents happy to escape the gloomy Washington weather. Dwight Eisenhower first landed in Palm Springs in February 1954, and the reason was to play golf. There were just two eighteen-hole courses there at the time, and Ike played both, because he loved golf—as presidents generally do, regardless of their other qualities.

On the night of February 20, something happened, something still unexplained. Eisenhower disappeared from Smoke Tree Ranch, the elaborate estate owned by Paul Helms, of Helms Bakery in Culver City. The White House press corps could not get a straight story.

In the confusion that followed, the Associated Press put out a ten-bell bulletin announcing that President Eisenhower was dead: "President Eisenhower died tonight of a heart attack in Palm Springs."

Just two minutes later, the bulletin was retracted. It was a mistake, the newswire explained. A lack of information had brought on an international panic.

A well-known local dentist, Francis A. Purcell, was later credited with repairing a broken crown on the president's front left incisor—tooth number 11. The president, according to the White House, had broken the crown while eating fried chicken and was hurried away for a secret dental visit.

But Dr. Purcell, later a founding board member of the College of the Desert, had no records of the procedure and could recall no details. Dr. and Mrs. Purcell had no trouble remembering the president's "steak fry" they attended the following day.

A strange story emerged in the months and years after Ike's 1954 holiday here, a story that fits in well with the Cold War UFO panic that had gripped America in the 1950s. Over several weeks in July 1952, unknown aerial craft appeared over Washington National Airport and the U.S. Capitol, both visually and on radar screens at Washington National and Andrews Air Force Base.

The mystery craft were seen by pilots and flight crews, from aircraft and from the ground. When fighter jets were scrambled, the fast-moving objects vanished from the sky, only to return when the fighter jets landed for refueling. General Eisenhower himself had seen a brilliant white craft appear alongside the USS *Franklin D. Roosevelt*—the first American ship armed with nuclear weapons—that same year, the year before he was inaugurated as president. He was on deck in the night, having a cup of coffee and a late-night cigarette, wearing his pajamas and robe. And then the NATO commander joined an excited group of sailors watching the UFO hovering a hundred feet over the ocean's surface. He left the sailors with instructions to "forget about this for now" and said he would check it out. All of which adds texture to the persistent story of Eisenhower's secret emergency the night of February 20, 1954: a late-night visit to Muroc Air Force Base, on the western edge of the Mojave Desert, for a diplomatic meeting with alien visitors.

Muroc is now known as Edwards Air Force Base, home of the "Right Stuff" pilots, with its dry-lake runway where the space shuttle often landed, where the fastest American aircraft were tested. But from the beginning of the dry lake's use as a natural runway, other aircraft appeared: mysterious things that would chase pilots through the night sky, or hover brazenly over the main runway, brilliant lights flashing every color. Then the mystery craft would rapidly accelerate to forty thousand or fifty thousand feet, when the fighter jets approached. In 1954, the leader of the free world was allegedly taken by helicopter to the Mojave Desert air base for a brief and symbolically important meeting with the space aliens—a diplomatic meeting with an intelligence that had baffled the armies of the world for centuries, but especially since World War II, and especially since the use of nuclear weapons on the previously primitive Earth.

The story emerged just seven weeks later, when a report of the encounter was sent to California's best-known UFO researcher, the Borderland Sciences Research

Associates director Meade Layne, in San Diego. Dignitaries were said to have been brought to the desert base with Ike, including the Los Angeles archbishop James McIntyre and the Truman-era White House economic adviser Edwin Nourse.

There, along with the president, they allegedly saw recovered craft. Recovered alien craft, of five different shapes and sizes.

On this single winter's night in the California desert in 1954, President Dwight D. Eisenhower is reported to have died of a heart attack, received secret medical treatment for dental work damaged by a bite of chicken, witnessed recovered UFOs in the Mojave, and made diplomatic contact with a race of space aliens.

Proceedings

OF THE
COLLEGE OF UNIVERSAL WISDOM
YUCCA VALLEY, CALIFORNIA

A BRANCH OF THE MINISTRY OF UNIVERSAL WISDOM, INC.

A Non-sectarian and Non-profit Organization

for Religious and Scientific Research.

VOLUME 11   JULY - AUGUST - SEPTEMBER - 1976   NUMBER 2

THE "INTEGRATRON", AND YOUR DIRECTORS HOME BESIDE IT, AS VIEWED FROM THE AIR.

THE KRILL PAPERS

As the southwestern United States began to boom in population during World War II, a mythology of UFOs and alien life grew up alongside the Sunbelt suburbs of America. Under clear, starry skies and surrounded by vast military bases, the new residents of sprawling cities such as Albuquerque, Phoenix, Las Vegas, and Los Angeles had to get used to aspects of life unknown in the Midwest or on the East Coast.

The adobe and pueblo styles of architecture were adapted, along with the decorative arts (if not the spiritual culture) of desert tribes. Roadrunners, scorpions, coyotes, and longhorn skulls became icons of the New West. And from the Lubbock Lights to the strange craft buzzing around the Lockheed Skunk Works in Lancaster, the reality of wondrous sights in the open skies led to a new paranoid culture fueled by the Cold War and the movie-screen UFOs produced by L.A. science fiction writers.

Intelligence agencies and defense contractors did not passively witness this new culture. Instead, the "alphabet agencies" and their black-project corporate partners actively engaged with the "contactees," prophets, and pulp writers, encouraging belief in both benevolent "space brothers" and hostile invaders.

When thousands of Americans began attending UFO conferences in the Mojave Desert, most notably at the Integratron builder George Van Tassel's compound at Giant Rock, spies from both Washington and Moscow mingled with the believers, planting new stories and new layers in what rapidly became a pop religion for these unanchored citizens of the desert cities.

Secret aircraft—from the first U-2 and SR-71 Blackbird to modern stealth bombers and fighters—were explained away as UFOs, especially when they crashed. Better to muddy the waters with outrageous tales than let classified details surface in daily newspapers and on the local television news.

Watergate, the House Select Committee on Assassinations, and the Church Committee added sinister new elements to the flying saucer stories of the 1970s. If the U.S. government could assassinate its own people or drive them to suicide with heavy dosages of hallucinogens, could they also be cooperating with extraterrestrial forces?

The Roswell crash, only briefly noticed by the national media in 1947 and just as quickly forgotten when the army explained the "crashed flying disk" as a failed weather balloon, was resuscitated in 1978 by a new group of UFO researchers ready to find a deeper conspiracy. In 1980, the first book-length examination of Roswell was published, thirty-three years after the events of 1947. *The Roswell Incident* was credited to Charles Berlitz and William L. Moore, and more or less created the mythology that would inspire scores of movies, TV shows, additional books, and websites on the early Internet.

When a murky "government source" supplied Bill Moore with photographs of supposed World War II–era documents from a secret UFO task force in Washington called MJ-12, it fueled belief in government complicity in a long-term colonization effort by extraterrestrial civilizations.

The 1980s brought new forms of media—dozens of cable channels, a fourth broadcast network, and the connection of millions of new personal computers to bulletin boards, newsgroups, and early consumer online services such as CompuServe and GEnie—that were ideal for spreading both sincere reports and "fake news." Melodramatic syndicated series about government cover-ups of alien crashes (*In Search Of . . .* , *Arthur C. Clarke's Mysterious World*) led to prime-time faux documentaries based mostly on fraudulent film and video. Movies and TV dramas made use of tropes from old UFO sightings and cover-ups. New eyewitness reports echoed the fictional stories. And a real-life character named Milton William Cooper made himself a prominent UFO researcher.

Cooper, born in 1943 in Long Beach, California, served in the navy during the Vietnam years and made a living at local technical schools before emerging with wild UFO conspiracies in the 1980s. By 1988, Cooper was—along with Bill Moore—part of a small group of middle-aged men who dominated the alien-conspiracy scene. They appeared on television and late-night radio talk shows such as Billy Goodman's weeknight Las Vegas broadcast (which paved the way for Art Bell's mainstream success in the 1990s), and they were busy contributors to online message boards such as ParaNet. Cooper eventually blew his credibility within that insular scene, and would find a new audience with his deeply paranoid New World Order conspiracies. His 1991 book *Behold a Pale Horse* became a guide for the militia movement and inspiration to a young Alex Jones, the Illuminati-obsessed Texas radio host who now counsels Donald Trump. But before Bill Cooper changed his focus from aliens to the deeply paranoid and lonesome emptiness of middle-aged American men like himself—and before he died in a November 2001 shootout with sheriff's deputies in Apache County, Arizona—he added to his UFO work by popularizing the Krill Papers, credited to the mysterious "O. H. Krill."

The Krill Papers confirmed everyone's worst fears: The government knew about the aliens, and the aliens had the upper hand.

It hardly mattered that John Lear, the retired pilot and son of the business-jet pioneer Bill Lear, had long admitted to circulating the Krill texts. Lear has said his friend John Grace, an air force officer then based at Nellis AFB, just north of Las Vegas, wrote this 1988 "estimate of the situation" based on sincere theories and beliefs regarding alien bases beneath U.S. government installations in Nevada and New Mexico.

Upon receiving the Krill Papers, Cooper immediately began claiming *he* had first read them way back in 1972, supposedly while serving in naval intelligence. Cooper apparently felt no embarrassment when Lear told him the documents had actually been written sixteen years later, as Cooper continued spreading this tall tale—notably on Billy Goodman's midnight broadcast, on a clear signal heard across the western United States.

John Lear has had a curious second career in the late-night world of UFO bulletin boards and call-in talk shows. But he has more or less consistently maintained that the Krill Papers reflect the bizarre truth, and are not a hoax. The only "joke," Lear has written on the Above Top Secret website, is in the name: In the 1950s, it was rumored that an alien pilot held by the U.S. military was known as CRLLL (these aliens apparently lack vowels in their names). The initials "O.H." meant nothing in particular, although Internet sleuths have since decided they stand for "Original Hostage."

If the Krill Papers have a familiar feel today, it's because they've fed the paranoid mythology that has become modern American culture.

THE KRILL PAPERS
O. H. KRILL

Craft from other worlds have crashed on Earth.

Alien craft are from both ultra-dimensional sources and sources within this dimension.

Early U.S. government efforts at acquiring alien technology were successful.

The U.S. government has had live alien hostages at some point in time.

The government has conducted autopsies on alien cadavers.

U.S. intelligence agencies, security agencies, and public agencies are involved in the cover-up of facts pertaining to the situation.

People have been and are currently being abducted, mutilated, murdered, and kidnapped as a result of the UFO situation.

There is a current active alien presence among us on this planet, which controls different elements of our society.

Alien forces maintain bases on Earth and on the moon.

Millions of cattle have been killed in the process of acquiring biological materials.

The U.S. government has had a working relationship with alien forces for some time, with the express purpose of gaining technology in gravitational propulsion, beam weaponry, and mind control.

DR. JAEGER'S HIBERNATING BIRD

The common poorwill (or Nuttall's Poor-Will) is a bird of great mystery and strange habits. The smallest of the nightjar hunters and a close relative of the owl, the poorwill prefers wide open spaces in the deserts and mountains of the west, making a simple nest from nothing more than a few scratches in the sandy ground.

When the full moon comes, the poorwill hunts all night through. Otherwise, the large-eyed bird hunts only in the first and last hours of darkness, when there is enough illumination to see the moths and beetles and other such insects that provide its nourishment.

Poorwill eggs are known to hatch at the full moon, allowing the father extra time to catch more bugs for the hungry hatchlings—the mother bird stays at the nest.

If the poorwill is disturbed while keeping its eggs warm or precocial young protected, it will tumble away from the nest and open its shockingly large mouth in apparent imitation of a snake, while making a convincing hissing sound. Here is a bird that has not forgotten its dinosaur heritage.

Being a well-camouflaged night hunter of the arid lands, the poorwill remains mysterious. Seen on the ground in twilight with its scale-like mottled feathers, it looks more like a horned lizard than an owl. Much is still unknown about the species' mating habits, real numbers, or exact family tree. Four desert subspecies, including the dusky poorwill and desert poorwill of California, are of "dubious validity." They migrate, unless they don't, while the migration of some common poorwills consists of heading up from the valleys to the mountains in summer, like mule deer or the seasonal staff at Furnace Creek.

Until the nineteenth century, the whippoorwill call was believed to belong to the nighthawk—another nightjar altogether. In ancient times, the bizarre nightjars were called goatsuckers because of the widespread belief that the birds feasted from the teats of goats in the night.

The common poorwill and the eastern whippoorwill were long presumed to be close kin, but that family bond has recently been ripped apart by the ornithologists. These taxonomy battles continue, with "eared nightjars" lately separated from the earless goatsuckers, while other bird experts say the whole gang belongs with the owls.

It was only in 1946 that a scientist first encountered a poorwill in such a state of torpor that it was originally presumed dead.

A century ago, the first white settlers to the Palm Springs area were in the canyons—Palm Canyon, Chino Canyon—where you had some shade and fresh water, hot springs for winter soaking, a perfect oasis.

For many centuries prior, this had been home to the Cahuilla people, the Agua Caliente tribe. Today the tribe owns fifty square miles of the Coachella Valley, from Palm Springs to Rancho Mirage, the land beneath twenty thousand homes and businesses, land still leased from the tribe today. One of the few good deals Native Americans got.

Anglo-Americans showed up during the gold rush, and by the early 1900s the first of the Palm Springs health resorts opened, catering to the "lungers"—those suffering from tuberculosis, wealthy people who came to the desert for the dry air and the mineral baths, in the time before the antibiotic cure was discovered in 1949.

There was another kind of Anglo-American resident, a new kind of eccentric called the "desert rat." And desert rats loved this landscape, loved the extremes of this land we call the Colorado Desert, meaning the part of the Sonoran Desert west of the Colorado River.

These desert rats were artists and philosophers, misfits and outlaws, generally not very fond of busy cities and the busy work of American life. They were talented painters and writers, and they included a strange character named Edmund Jaeger—Dr. Jaeger, as he is remembered today, the pioneering desert biologist.

He lived in a wooden shack in Palm Canyon and he

traveled these desert lands his whole adult life, making great discoveries, including the discovery, in 1946, of the first-known hibernating bird, the common poorwill, which he found sleeping away the winter months in a little nook along the rock walls east of Palm Springs, a place now protected as a nature sanctuary in the Chuckwalla Mountains. Visit in the cold months, if you go. It's beautiful, and just an hour's drive east from the now-busy Coachella Valley.

Dr. Jaeger was not fooled by the bird's apparent lack of life. Handling the small nightjar, Dr. Jaeger suspected torpor, otherwise unknown in birds. The sleepy poorwill slowly opened one eye, peering up at the desert biologist.

The comatose bird had first been noticed by Dr. Jaeger's hiking companion that day. It was lying within a shallow granite niche not very far above the ground. Dr. Jaeger banded the bird and returned it to the niche. Many return visits to this quiet spot confirmed that the bird remained in a state of torpor for more than eighty days, even through a violent winter storm that had frayed the poorwill's tail feathers during its long slumber.

What appeared to be hibernating common poorwills had been observed 140 years earlier by Meriwether Lewis, of the Lewis and Clark expedition, but the importance was lost in the reams of data from the expedition. Lewis misidentified the bird as an eastern whippoorwill, too; the species had not yet been separated by ornithologists. By studying the mysterious nightjar for three successive winters, Dr. Jaeger documented the seasonal patterns of this strange behavior for the first time. That this lone poorwill would return to the very same uncomfortable, exposed dip in a cold rock wall, winter after winter, was almost too weird. But poorwills are weird by nature.

They are utterly indifferent to the heat of the day, often nesting in open, sun-blasted stretches of hardened sand. They eat large insects whole and expel the exoskeletons in owl-like pellets. They seem utterly indifferent to comfort of any kind.

They live alone or in nesting pairs but often hunt in large groups, erratically flitting through the dusk like bats. If the names "poorwill" and "nightjar" seem wrong for the species, you can always call them by their old common name, "bullbat." Are those large bats flapping around your head on an evening hike, or are they bullbats? There is a clue in the nightjar's awful croak. In *Birds of the Great Basin: A Natural History*, author Fred A. Ryser noted that the poorwill's obnoxious call "does sound somewhat like the bellowing of a bull."

The Hopi have always called the common poorwill

hölchko, "the sleeping one," as Dr. Jaeger points out. And his later friendship with a Navajo rancher revealed that torpid poorwills were routinely discovered in the Navajo Nation highlands by shepherds.

"On December 20, 1947, Mr. Joseph Brauner kindly sent me two centigrade thermometers, one slow-registering, the other quick-registering," Dr. Jaeger wrote in the May–June 1949 issue of the esteemed ornithology journal *The Condor*. This fine scientific equipment was put to rigorous use, as Dr. Jaeger explained in great detail:

> With these and thermometers of my own I began taking a series of rectal temperatures every fourteen days. The feather-insulated bird was held in the hand and the bulb of the thermometer was thrust into the coprodaeum and into the rectum to a depth of one-and-a-half inches. There the instrument was held until the reading became constant; usually this was achieved in three minutes.

Nearly two decades later, at the end of 1964, the astounding discovery and documentation of the hibernating poorwill was acknowledged with the creation of the Edmund C. Jaeger Nature Sanctuary.

Visiting the Edmund C. Jaeger Nature Sanctuary today also means paying your respects to the late Dr. Jaeger, who died at the age of ninety-six back in 1983. The cremated remains of the pioneering desert biologist were scattered by his friends in the very slot canyon where that single hibernating common poorwill was first discovered and watched over for three successive desert winters in the 1940s.

THE DEVIL (?) IN AMBOY CRATER

Out on Route 66, in the heart of the Mojave Desert, there's a big black cinder cone rising from the scorched earth about fifty miles from anywhere. It's called Amboy Crater, and it scares the kind of people who tend to believe whatever they hear.

The crater doesn't bother desert rats, of course. *They* like the place. They'll go out there on a June afternoon about three months past the "nice time of year" and crunch through the sand and lava rock to the rim of the 250-foot-tall extinct volcano, and then they'll just march right down into the pit of the thing, where the basalt last settled in pools about ten thousand years ago, at the end of the Pleistocene, when Lake Mojave and Lake Manix covered much of the land to the north of Amboy and the whole region was wetter, greener, and abundant with enormous animals.

When the paving of U.S. Route 66 was completed in 1935, Amboy Crater became a tourist attraction for those enjoying a desert crossing on their way to Los Angeles.

Those traveling the "Mother Road" in hopes of escaping the poverty and desperation of the Dust Bowl must've looked upon the dead black volcano with dread. When would the California of magazines and movie screens appear? Never, for most of the "Okies" headed to the cotton fields and oil rigs of Bakersfield. But that is another story, best told by the works of John Steinbeck and Merle Haggard.

For those braving the Mojave for pleasure, a scramble up the cinder cone was a way to brag of having conquered a real-life volcano, followed by cold drinks or ice cream at Roy's Cafe, the busiest spot between Barstow and Needles—especially after World War II, when the rationing of gasoline and tire rubber came to an end and Southern Californians enjoyed a golden age of recreational motoring over mountains and desert.

Roy's was open around the clock by the 1950s, employing seventy people at the café, filling station, garage, and motel. In those busy days began the modern legends of Amboy Crater.

The distinct odor of sulfur was reported at the crater's floor, especially in the hours following Southern California earthquakes. Geologic explanations were of little interest to those looking for the devil's influence, as those wild spots on Earth that "smell like hell" have often made their way into mythology. When Interstate 40 opened on a route twenty miles north of Roy's in 1972, Amboy was left without the travelers that sustained it. Herman "Buster" Burris, cofounder of Roy's with his father-in-law, Roy Crowl, was a cantankerous old desert character by the time I-40 killed his business. It is said he bulldozed half the town, such was his disgust after Route 66 became a ghost road.

Burris was openly hostile to his only regular customers once the interstate opened: long-haired motorcycle riders doing weekend runs on old Route 66. Were those leering bikers from San Bernardino and Fontana affiliated with Charles Manson's old gang? It seemed prudent to assume so, and wasn't Charles Manson born and raised right there in Amboy, anyway?

He was not. The murder-cult leader and race-war proponent was born in Cincinnati to an alcoholic hillbilly mother from across the river in Ashland, Kentucky, who tried and failed to trade five-year-old Charlie for a beer. There are stories—there are *always* stories about the Manson Family—that he spent part of his grim childhood in the *New Jersey* town of Amboy. It's a story, at least. As for persistent rumors that Manson camped out around Amboy Crater at some point in his grim career, they're likely influenced by his known desert haunts, especially Barker Ranch on the western flank of the Panamints, at the end of a steep dirt road about an hour south of Ballarat and just within the boundary of Death Valley National Park.

It was here that Manson and his Family were captured on October 12, 1969, following the seven ritual murders in Los Angeles, although sheriff's deputies arrived at the remote property looking only for car thieves: Manson initially faced auto-theft charges at the Inyo County Courthouse, on Highway 395, in the Eastern Sierra town of Independence.

There are lingering suspicions that the Manson

gang was responsible for still-unsolved murders in Olancha and Bishop, and 2008 saw a new forensic dig at Barker Ranch. But the Amboy connection exists only in folklore.

Long before the "Helter Skelter" rampage made Charles Manson the archetypal lunatic hiding out in the desert, there were reported cases of "isolation nerves" getting the best of people in Amboy. In the late 1930s, bored youths gathered the remnants of blown tires and other highway rubbish and proceeded to set it all aflame at the bottom of the cinder cone. The black smoke from the burning rubber convinced the small town's residents that the volcano had come back to life, and many townspeople grabbed a suitcase and rushed to their vehicles to escape the eruption.

A peculiar "Satanic Panic" gripped California in the 1980s, fueled by cable-television preachers and a general intellectual decline still much in evidence across America. Most anything unfamiliar to the suburban population of the Golden State was quickly categorized as satanic, with local TV newscasters quick to spread the tales, whether about neighborhood preschools or rock-band graffiti at desert campsites. Even the muck left behind by fishermen and deer hunters could spark a mini-mob on the hunt for the ever-elusive satanic killers.

An example of this paranoia was noted at Amboy Crater by a self-described "treasure hunter" named William White. Encountering a group of "middle class" hikers or geology students enjoying the crater's famous cinder cone on a pleasant autumn day in 1988, White and his son decided the people were satanists—because they weren't riding off-road vehicles, and because they weren't brandishing firearms, as White apparently did as a matter of practice when visiting such natural attractions.

"There were no smiles to be seen anywhere," wrote White. "Only frowns and malevolent stares coming from this group. There was also the absence of desert toys. No dirt bikes or quads could be seen. Just what were these people doing here anyway?"

Gosh, who would go to a protected natural area on public lands and forget their *dirt bikes and firearms*? Somehow, the sight of a couple of heavily armed fellows scowling from an out-of-state truck did not charm the visitors at Amboy Crater. They seemed no happier when White drove ("slowly") right through the group, but it was his lucky day and the mysterious pedestrians didn't pursue him on foot.

White and his son finally emerged from their vehicle and trudged up the trail. To White's delight, his son found (or created) a pentagram scrawled in the dust at the bottom of the crater.

"They were devil worshipers for sure and we had

just crashed their party," White concludes in his *True Treasure Stories of the Southwest*. "The scary part of it was that these people looked like normal citizens." Normal but for their lack of off-road vehicles, anyway.

Some two dozen feature films have used Amboy as a location, mostly low-budget thrillers. Along with the semiliterate Internet message boards that create and maintain modern American myths, late-night cable fare such as *Live Evil* and *Devil Girl* feed Amboy's haunted reputation.

WHEN THE NIGHTS WERE WEIRD: ART BELL AND THE KINGDOM OF NYE

In its 1990s prime, the late-night radio show *Coast to Coast AM* was an unscripted audio mix of *Twin Peaks* and *The X-Files*. It was uncomfortable, laughable, utterly paranoid, completely of its time, and occasionally terrifying.

Because it was broadcast in the middle of the night, if you listened it was generally because you were alone: driving a deserted highway, or fighting insomnia, or working a graveyard shift under fluorescent lights. A parade of oddballs told their tales each night, people seemingly lacking even a basic sense of humor, all of them explaining conspiracies both obvious and fantastic. And then, because this was also the golden age of weirdness on the early World Wide Web, you could look up these radio characters and discover that "Major Ed Dames," for example, really was a retired military officer who really did "remote viewing" for a secret government project called "Stargate," which was also apparently a real thing. This was always the terrifying part about the show: Some of it, maybe all of it, was *true*.

Behind it all was exactly the kind of person you were told to avoid in real life: Art Bell, a chain-smoking hermit and deejay with a sinister laugh who worked from a mobile-home compound in the High Desert just west of Nevada's Area 51, the most notorious "secret government base" of all.

In October 1998, at the peak of his fame, Bell announced the first of a bewildering series of retirements from *Coast to Coast AM*. Five years later, the weeknight broadcast was handed over to a midwestern radio personality named George Noory, who still hosts the late-night show from Premiere Networks' studios in Los Angeles. The program has lost the lonely desert feel that made it so unique, although the veteran paranormal reporter George Knapp can occasionally be heard guest-hosting on Sunday nights from Las Vegas.

Bell's many retirements, perhaps a dozen in all, had just about been accepted by his aging fans when another surprise appeared, this time on his Facebook page. "I am now in negotiation for a new Radio show," he posted from Pahrump in January 2013. "No promises, but the wind may be about to change direction!"

It was always vague and mysterious with Art Bell, who could make the most innocuous subject—such as where his cats were hiding in his home studio on any given night—carry the emotional dread of annihilation by extraterrestrial invaders. The jarring transition from voyeuristic amusement to lock-the-doors paranoia was the peak experience for the Art Bell listener. And that was the reason to keep listening.

Art Bell is tragic proof that fame and fortune cannot guarantee a pleasurable life. He first quit the radio show at the height of its popularity, in the late 1990s, reportedly because some local psychopath had sexually assaulted Bell's young son with the stated goal of infecting the boy with HIV. In 2006, Bell's third wife, Ramona, died, in the couple's RV, when it was parked outside a casino-motel in Laughlin, the kind of place where you could still find nickel slots and half the clientele dragged portable oxygen canisters behind them. He apparently sat around his Mojave Desert compound for a while, after the death of Ramona Bell, and then decided to move to the Philippines and marry a girl he met over the Internet. He finally came back to Pahrump, but immigration problems kept his fourth wife out of the United States for many years.

Bell had a thick file full of health problems by his forties, including a severe back injury from falling off a telephone pole and the many ailments that follow the lifetime chain-smoker.

For all of his very public misfortunes, Bell had the best voice on radio and a master's touch with the callers and guests. The show was pure suspense, delivered in reliable nightly doses of jarringly unexpected-yet-expected moments that would scare the listener into another two hours of insomnia, hearing every nighttime sound of a settling house as an invasion of sinister entities.

To listen during an actual, unfolding regional freakout was the best kind of Art Bell–era *Coast to Coast AM* program. During the 1997 Phoenix Lights incident, listeners in Nevada and Arizona called in with eyewitness descriptions of the gigantic black craft moving silently over highways and exurbs. A Texan private pilot calling in by mobile phone from a small plane once described his flight across Area 51's restricted airspace. And a convincingly frantic "former employee" at the fabled Dreamland base described subterranean halls teeming with escaped interdimensional beings—and then, of course, the phone call cuts off and Art Bell's entire broadcast briefly goes off the air.

Callers were divided by geography: "East of the Rockies, West of the Rockies," Bell would announce with the gravity of Johnny Cash. There were special toll-free numbers for both sides of the country, along with pop-up numbers for specific classes of paranormal incident, or for military personnel and highway patrol officers who had witnessed a certain type of unidentified flying object.

They were paintings in sound, these 1990s broadcasts. While the Internet existed, it existed more or less within a vacuum of limited and crudely amateur "content." Nor could you simply go to Google Maps and look at close-range satellite imagery of the Groom Lake airfield, as anyone with a cell phone can do today. But you *could* find the dubious UFO images and alien-conspiracy text files so often referenced on the shows by the guests and callers.

Art Bell sounded out of time even when he was on

the air live. The old ABBA hit "Dancing Queen" was often the "bumper music" separating Bell's Kingdom of Nye (County) from the banal network news on the hour. *Coast to Coast*'s advertising frequently consisted of Bell—a longtime ham radio operator—lovingly describing the circuitry within the C. Crane Company's tabletop radios. If you're lucky, you can catch one of these old recorded broadcasts on a late-night desert drive, as part of the aptly named *Somewhere in Time* repeats that Premiere still airs on Saturday nights. They sound best on a scratchy AM station a few states over, as you glance around the suddenly ominous night sky.

And that's how Art Bell is still with us today: a ghost of Saturday night, a fading memory of static and terror, because his return to radio in the autumn of 2013 completely imploded shortly after it began. His new show, *Dark Matters*, lasted just six weeks on SiriusXM satellite radio before a bizarre feud with management ended the much-publicized return of the late-night master of the AM waves. A last attempt occurred in 2015, for a new show called *Midnight in the Desert*. But six months later, Art Bell had retired for the very last time.

Bell passed away at home in Pahrump on April 13, 2018.

THE GOVERNOR'S SPACE ALIEN

The key witness to 1997's Phoenix Lights events was Arizona's governor at the time, Fife Symington, who saw an "enormous" silent black triangle pass overhead at low altitude on the night of March 13.

"It just felt otherworldly," Governor Symington told CNN. "In your gut, you could just tell it was otherworldly."

Symington was in his second term on the night thousands of people, from Nevada to the Mexican state of Sonora, reported seeing massive, silent craft looming over highway traffic, small desert towns, and especially the vast Phoenix metropolitan area.

But Symington didn't tell CNN about his emotionally overwhelming sighting of this "otherworldly" craft until a decade afterward—by which time he was out of politics. As a former air force captain, Symington could have added tremendously to the credibility of the eyewitness pool, and his report might have offered comfort to the vast numbers of Arizona's citizens who saw ominous things floating slowly overhead.

Instead, after weeks of increasing hysteria and a

surge of national press coverage, Symington called reporters to the state capital, Phoenix, and played a prank on them.

With television crews broadcasting the press conference to both local news stations and CNN, Symington solemnly declared that state officials "had found who was responsible" for the panic. And then his security guards brought out an "alien," in the form of Symington's chief of staff in a Halloween costume. The response from the press was a few forced, sycophantic chuckles. The news organizations ceased coverage; there are always other oddities requiring a few days of attention.

When asked why he withheld his own sighting for ten years and instead ridiculed those who admitted seeing the craft, Symington blamed his own "panic," and said he wanted to deflate lingering unease that he feared might escalate into a total breakdown of society.

"As a public figure," he told CNN in 2007, "you have to be very careful what you say, because people can have pretty emotional reactions."

Symington now claims that he did his best to solve the riddle in the skies, but the commanders at Arizona's military air bases told him they were as "perplexed" as the other witnesses.

The first black triangle of the evening was reportedly seen over the Las Vegas suburb of Henderson. Witnesses next saw the mysterious behemoth over the Prescott Valley, and then it began its widely seen northwest-to-southeast crossing over Phoenix and the desert beyond. It was last reported over Sonora, Mexico.

When the reports were tallied, several variations of the craft were noted—often in very specific detail. There were higher-altitude formations of lights flying in V patterns, dark silent craft the size of commercial jets, and, most shockingly, detailed eyewitness reports of impossibly gigantic black craft moving low and slow and seemingly right on top of people. Drivers who pulled over on Interstate 10 reported helplessly crouching down, as the enormous thing seemed close enough to touch.

A second event, long suspected as the intentional release of military flares over the Estrella Mountains, south of Phoenix, around 10:00 p.m., began more than an hour after the triangular craft had crossed the sprawling city and had already appeared over Tucson, apparently heading south. As word of the original sighting spread from neighbor to neighbor and then led the local television news, throngs of people went outside to search the night sky for mysterious lights.

And they were rewarded with a string of fizzling golden orbs familiar to anyone who lives within view of a southwestern military base. The easily explained flares—which may *not* have been flares, either—were conflated with reports of the giant craft. The governor paraded his Halloween-costumed employee before the assembled media, and the Phoenix Lights became another part of American folklore to be endlessly rehashed by the paranormal documentaries on cable television. As for the black triangles often seen hovering over desert highways to this day, they are usually explained away as some as-yet-unknown top-secret military aircraft.

Why they are so brightly lit—and flown so brazenly over roads and towns—has not been satisfactorily explained.

But if you travel the old Mojave Road alongside Manix Wash, just west of Afton Canyon, you'll find these familiar black triangles upon the scorched rocky mesa just above the historic trail. The dark triangles are geoglyphs, or *intaglios*, made long ago by the old ones who frequented this ancient desert highway.

BROADCASTS FROM BEYOND

Transmissions come in many ways: weird lights in the desert brush for Moses, circles of multicolored fire in the sky for Ezekiel, a column of fire for the wanderers in the wilderness. Baffling bright lights over the desert highway, over the road to Damascus. The beam of pink light that set off years of strange visions and prophecies in Philip K. Dick. A column of light that bathed a thirteen-year-old French girl as voices spoke strange prophecy. She would become known to the world as Joan of Arc.

A light turns on in your brain, that's how the big ideas arrive. *I have seen the light.*

The Virgin of Fátima was an entity of blinding white light, communicating wordlessly to three shepherd children, the children who promised and delivered a miracle for the masses on October 13, 1917. When tens of thousands arrived at this Portuguese town, they witnessed something brighter than the sun appearing on the overcast day, seemingly below the clouds, with rain drenching an immense crowd standing in the mud. An eyewitness described the encounter:

"This was not the sparkling of a heavenly body, for it spun round on itself in a mad whirl, when suddenly a clamor was heard from all the people. The sun, whirling, seemed to loosen itself from the firmament, and advance threateningly upon the earth as if to crush us with its huge fiery weight. The sensation during those moments was terrible."

That eyewitness report comes from José Garrett, a lawyer and son of a science professor. Reporters from Paris and London witnessed the bizarre phenomena, which included the muddy pastures and standing rainwater turning to warm dry ground in a matter of minutes. The sodden clothing of the multitudes was instantly dried by the intense heat radiated by the spinning disc hovering just above a crowd of more than forty thousand, many of them recoiling from the spectacle and the waves of heat, many more kneeling in prayer or wailing in terror.

The Great War, World War I, would end the following summer with sixteen million people dead, in the trenches, by genocide, and by starvation. But another fifty million people would lose their lives to the Spanish flu pandemic that began in the spring of 1918. Two of the three "Fátima children," Francisco and Jacinta Marto, would die of the pandemic, leaving only Lúcia dos Santos—the peasant girl who was ordered by the entity to become literate in order to write down the Three Secrets of Fátima.

Illumination is the process of enlightenment. Long before Thomas Edison claimed credit for inventing the lightbulb, a beam of light or brilliant flame from a candle or lantern illustrated knowledge, wisdom, initiation. The lights dancing upon the heads of the apostles on the Pentecost. For Hank Williams, that light fell upon his head while he was being driven home from a honky-tonk performance, "like a stranger in the night. Praise the Lord, I saw the light."

Václav Havel, the Czech playwright who led his nation to freedom from the Warsaw Pact and Soviet Union, describes in *Letters to Olga* how he was sitting in a prison yard, staring idly at a tree he had seen hundreds of times before, when the sunlight struck the leaves in the breeze in such a way that he went into a trance. He was forever changed.

But not completely: He had already chosen a hard road. He was an author, a playwright turned human-rights activist, and his political action had already robbed him of a comfortable intellectual's life, had made him a prisoner in a prison yard while his nation suffocated. This encounter with the divine gave him new strength.

"I felt a sense of reconciliation, of an almost gentle consent to the inevitable course of things as revealed to me now, and this combined with a carefree determination to face what had to be faced." This is Havel, writing from prison to his wife, Olga. "This joy formed a strange alliance in me, with a vague horror at the unattainability of everything I was so close to . . . In that moment, I would even say that I was somehow struck by love, though I don't know precisely for whom or what."

Decades later, having fulfilled his destiny, having

gone to the castle and then returned to private life, Havel described how such encounters "slumber in our collective unconscious":

> These experiences surface again and again in the cultural achievements of humanity—and often in individual human experiences as well. In a way that we scarcely understand, they transcend what a person might know in himself or inherit from his ancestors. It seems rather as if something like an antenna were picking up signals from a physically indeterminable transmitter that contains the experience of the entire human race.

Philip K. Dick called it VALIS: Vast Active Living Intelligence System. Carl Jung named it the collective unconscious. We don't know what it is, and we don't know if it's divinely inspired, because we can't agree on what "divine" means. But it's real and it's there and if you're hungry for knowledge, the gates will be found open, eventually, maybe when you're looking for it least—every door in the house of wisdom, open to all those who take the trouble to try the lock, twist the doorknob. The Kingdom of Heaven, the Earthly Paradise, is here among you, and so many cannot see it.

All of these contact types—religions, rituals, sacrifice, prayer, pleading—are protocols developed over tens of thousands of years. A loose priesthood exists among those who attempt such things. Those of us who open our eyes to see and ears to listen, listening for whatever is behind the blinding lights and the voices and the visions, the ghostly figures who walk through walls and bring the baffled human to the mystery ship hovering above, the little columns of machine elves marching around when we open a particular door in the mind, the kobold goblins who led medieval German miners to their deaths. The relationship is unsettled, unclear. From our side, anyway. Maybe it makes more sense from their side, maybe to some of them. Maybe they're us, from another time, from another dimension. They've always been right here with us on Earth. This is their home, too.

Our natural world functions as a supernatural habitat for an intelligence that has accompanied mankind since the beginning of our time, and has chosen to demonstrate itself (themselves?), on occasion, and possibly through great effort, great use of energy, light, electrical plasma, transmission of information and mood, directly to the contactee's consciousness.

Such contacts have always occurred at the wilderness-civilization interface, the frontier between the built environments of mankind and the natural earthly environments. The desert, especially.

The intelligence is deeply and significantly different from us. There is not a human alive who can tell you with certainty whether the intelligence is artificial, natural, generated by our own consciousness, generated by an external consciousness, extraterrestrial, or transdimensional. We don't know if it's "real" or something like the voice assistant on a mobile phone, clumsily misinterpreting our intent and giving us the wrong information most of the time.

The earthly names we have given such entities are just that: names, and not scientific descriptions. One person's god is another person's goblin. The shiny metallic craft reported by a military pilot might, in the eyes of an Axial Age prophet, be a brilliant chariot pulled by sky monsters. And neither are likely physical craft, things that exist in a stable state of matter or being. For more than seventy years the UFO cult has chased rumors of nuts-and-bolts interplanetary spacecraft visiting Earth from other solar systems, other galaxies, and we've got nothing to prove it, nothing to show for the effort.

But in that time, across those seven decades of technological marvels and spiritual collapse, *we* have constructed interplanetary spacecraft and *we* have visited and landed upon other worlds, moons and planets and asteroids. And with the twin *Voyager* craft, we have now traveled beyond our solar system. We have counted nearly four thousand exoplanets, the very first of those in the 1990s, only a quarter century ago. We, the Earth people, have computed a likely number of Earth-sized, potentially habitable planets, based on four thousand discovered planets and three thousand star systems detected by our space telescopes, and that number now stands at eleven billion planets—just in our own galaxy, the Milky Way.

Every human being alive today could have their

own habitable planet in the Milky Way, and four billion Earth-sized planets in the habitable zone could still be set aside as wilderness, galactic natural parks, spiritual and biological refuges.

If we don't kill off our own planet first, a galaxy of incredible adventure and discovery awaits humanity in the coming decades and centuries. We are closer to the likely time of human colonies on Mars and the moon than we are to World War II or *I Love Lucy* or "I Want to Hold Your Hand" or Watergate or Reagan vs. Carter.

Gods, E.T., devils, angels, ghosts, elves, pixies, chupacabras, Sasquatch, skin-walkers, sprites, reptilians, tall Nordics, grays, motherships, Mother Mary. Contacts in early human civilization established a protocol, a pantheon of tricksters and saviors and jealous gods demanding sacrifice and allegiance. And this protocol was built upon an ongoing process of revelation in the wild deserts, outside the great cities.

The founding of the great monotheistic religions, the modern and ancient folklore regarding rumored alien visitations, anthropological evidence such as petroglyphs and intaglios . . . the protocol is deeply attached to our species and is the basis for the limited and mysterious relationship we have with the intelligence or entities. The details and names change but the basics stay the same. As Jesus commanded his disciples: "Come ye yourselves apart into a desert place, and rest awhile." It was advice he himself repeatedly followed, alone in desert wilderness.

The evidence suggests the most fruitful place to continue the work of communication with the entities and intelligences is a physical and spiritual anchoring in the desert wilderness. We must act as part priesthood, part anthropologists. We engage in cleverness or deception at our peril and with no record of success. The last words you want to hear from a god are "the next time you see me coming, you better run."

The ongoing work is to study and disseminate occurrences of interest to students in this field. Cultures throughout history have created social structures to recognize those individuals who seem to be conduits of information or intent from the intelligence, from the entities. These occurrences may or may not display typical attributes of a religious or paranormal experience. They may exhibit their presence through the creation of strikingly beautiful and influential art, such as the New Mexico paintings of Georgia O'Keeffe. Or the matter-of-fact testimony from professional pilots after experiences with brilliant and intelligently controlled lights in the open sky.

Whether there are naturally evil or chaotic elements is unknown. Did Charles Manson receive sinister instructions? Or did his mind and spirit, ruined by human cruelty, pervert vague messages into instructions for setting off a global race war that he would wait out in the desert? What about the consistent appearance of death cults when society is fraying, the violent cults worshipping Kali the Destroyer and Santa Muerte, these returns to sacrificial rites, gifts to goddesses of death and destruction?

These events, across time and across cultures and largely across the deserts that make up one-third of our planet's landmass, should be remembered and studied with an open heart and an open mind, because they contain a code.

Not a numerical puzzle, not a riddle to be solved. The code consists of patterns and variations that may well add up to a revelation that comes seemingly out of the blue. It may concurrently occur around the world, as great scientific leaps are so often dreamed up at the same time by far-flung researchers—what is called multiple discovery or simultaneous independent invention. It's why Nobel prizes in the sciences so often are split between two or three researchers from different continents, from different universities, with different approaches. Serendipity, coincidence, synchronicity. What will it mean when we know how it works?

There are many good and noble reasons to protect the wilderness that remains, to be wise stewards of the only planet we've got at the moment. Keeping a wild, open landscape available for our encounters with the mysterious and the divine is as good a reason as the rest and maybe the best one of all.

Come on out and give it a try. Maybe you'll see a UFO. Maybe you'll see something weirder.

ACKNOWLEDGMENTS

Desert Oracle began in January 2015 because I needed a mission to occupy the rest of my life. Just enough people decided it was worth their time and dollars, and that's why the little periodical is still going, a half dozen years later. I am especially grateful for the patience of the print subscribers. Maybe I'll get caught up next year.

KCDZ FM's Gary Daigneault allowed me to take over Joshua Tree's only radio station on Friday nights, and Sara Snyder politely prods me for those new episodes so that the "Voice of the Desert" is heard on the airwaves from Amboy to Zzyzx, and across the Great Mojave Wilderness. Much of this book began as stories and sermons for *Desert Oracle Radio*. (If you want to hear the weekly program on your own community radio station, let us know, or get the show from Public Radio Exchange.)

RedBlueBlackSilver has created more than two hundred moodily beautiful soundscapes for the radio show and our occasional live events, and it has long been my dream to have this kind of instinctual musical collaboration.

The following editors kindly allowed me to write some of this book on somebody else's dime: Carolyn Kellogg, Kristin Sharkey, Steven Biller, and Kim Stringfellow. Extra thanks to Carolyn Kellogg for introducing me to Sean McDonald, publisher of MCD and now a frequent recipient of my late-night correspondence, through no fault of his own.

Doc Daniels, Rachel Monroe, Jay Babcock, Anna Merlan, Brendan Maze, Alana May Johnson, Jeremy Corbell, Cyrus Moqtaderi, Megan Mote, and Jason P. Woodbury have repeatedly contributed to the operation in various ways. Deborah Netburn got *Desert Oracle* on the front page of the *Los Angeles Times* way back in the summer of 2015, tripling our subscriber count overnight.

Magazine distributors were completely uninterested in a small journal about this endlessly fascinating part of North America, but individual bookshops and desert retailers stocked *Desert Oracle* on their own: Coyote Corner, Hoof and the Horn, Skylight Books, Issues Shop, Red Rock Books, 29 Palms Inn, Back of Beyond Books, The Station, Mincing Mockingbird, BKB Ceramics, and other such shops scattered across the Southwest introduced *Desert Oracle* to tens of thousands of desert residents and visitors.

To the readers and the radio listeners, the people who travel from distant lands to join me around a campfire for some stories and conversation and whiskey, and everyone who ever scribbled out a card or letter that wound up in P.O. Box 1735 out here in Joshua Tree, thanks for heeding the call.

> —**KEN LAYNE**
> Yucca Valley, California
> May 20, 2020

PHOTOGRAPH CREDITS

p. 46: U.S. Bureau of Land Management

p. 56: JPL-Caltech / NASA

p. 62: Tom Koerner, U.S. Fish & Wildlife

p. 74: Shutterstock

p. 86: Los Alamos Historical Society

p. 96: U.S. Bureau of Land Management

p. 124: Philip Harrington / Alamy Stock Photo

p. 232: U.S. Army

p. 254: Bob Wick, U.S. Bureau of Land Management

p. 262: Esther Bubley, U.S. Office of War Information

All other photographs are by the author.